THE DEBATE ABOUT THE BIBLE

THE DEBATE
ABOUT
THE BIBLE

Inerrancy Versus Infallibility

by
STEPHEN T. DAVIS

THE WESTMINSTER PRESS
PHILADELPHIA

Published by The Westminster Press®
Philadelphia, Pennsylvania

PRINTED IN THE UNITED STATES OF AMERICA

Library of Congress Cataloging in Publication Data

Davis, Stephen T   1940–
  The debate about the Bible.
  Bibliography: p.
  1. Bible—Evidences, authority, etc.
I. Title.
BS480.D32   220.1   77–3457
ISBN 0–664–24119–0

Do you believe the Scriptures of the Old and New Testaments to be the Word of God, the only infallible rule of faith and practice?

ANSWER: I do so believe.

From "Form and Order for the Ordination to the Holy Ministry," *The Book of Common Worship* (1946)

CONTENTS

FOREWORD

WHY SHOULD I, an evangelical theologian committed to the position of Biblical inerrancy which Dr. Davis is endeavoring to overturn, find it fitting to write the Foreword on its behalf, encouraging others to consider his thesis and arguments?

First, it is because I believe that there are many more ways than one to defend a high view of Biblical inspiration and authority, and that all of them should be tried. This is especially true in a climate in which some vocal evangelicals are suggesting that Warfield's doctrine of perfect errorlessness is the only sound position, and the alternative to it is liberalism and apostasy. This I consider divisive sectarianism. Therefore I am pleased rather than disconcerted when a work such as this appears. We need to listen to Dr. Davis, who strives to present a sturdy concept of Biblical authority without employing the category of inerrancy in it. The evangelical public needs to consider his thesis and to judge whether it is successful.

Second, the force of this unassuming book is to push the defenders of inerrancy to greater honesty and explicitness in their exposition of the concept. Dr. Davis shows inerrancy to be a much more subtle and com-

plex deduction about Scripture than it is commonly
believed to be. In many of its versions, he shows that
errors of various types are, in fact, admitted, and held
to be compatible with "inerrancy," which proves to be
a less obvious and straightforward notion than is generally acknowledged. The unspoken qualifications
which Dr. Davis uncovers in the theory will have to
be made more explicit in the future if its proponents
are to retain their full integrity. On the basis of full
disclosure a fruitful dialogue can begin to take place.

Third, the thesis will provide a pastoral service to
those who are troubled with marginal difficulties in the
Bible but are deeply committed to the evangelical
faith. The theory of perfect errorlessness when pressed
can leave such persons stranded with nothing to hold
on to if a single point however minute stands in any
doubt. This is a version of the "domino theory" we
should hear more about because it affects a large number of some of our finest people. Finding nowhere to
stand outside strict inerrancy, they cease to stand at all,
even on behalf of the great truths of the gospel which
stand with or without inerrancy.

I appreciate in Dr. Davis' work a level of profound
common sense operating. He reminds us that throughout the whole of church history believers have been
able to maintain their orthodox convictions despite the
fact, which no one contests, that the only Bible they
have possessed has been a fallible translation of fallible
manuscripts of Scripture. If that is true, surely some of
the heat hanging over this discussion should dissipate,
and a calmer, more serene spirit of inquiry replace it.

The fact that I believe that people ought to give Dr.
Davis a hearing does not mean I feel no uneasiness and

see no dangers in his proposal. He allows errors that are not "crucially relevant" to faith and practice. He acknowledges the Bible's authority until he meets a passage that "for good reasons" he cannot accept. I think I understand what Dr. Davis means by such expressions, and do not mistrust him personally in his application of them. However, I cannot look out over the theological landscape today and feel content for evangelicals to leave themselves so vulnerable and unguarded in their convictions about the Bible. I feel much happier myself with the strong but flexible wording of the Lausanne Covenant, "inerrant in all that it affirms," which can accommodate much of Dr. Davis' wisdom without leaving itself open to easy manipulation by those whose spirit is not docile before the teaching authority of the Word of God. I do not relish the prospect of evangelicals' handling the Bible the way liberals do—assigning certain texts to limbo while canonizing texts held to be more suitable and acceptable. It would be quite mistaken to suppose that, once rid of perfect errorlessness, we sail on a sea quite free of peril and controversy. Therefore I urge the reader to canvass this book carefully and critically, as well as patiently and sympathetically, so that he or she will receive the largest benefit from the effort of reading it.

CLARK H. PINNOCK

Vancouver, British Columbia

PREFACE

LET ME BEGIN with a perplexing fact. I consider myself an evangelical Christian. Yet there are persons
who, if they knew my beliefs, would deny that I am
truly evangelical. They would deny this on the
grounds that I do not affirm that the Bible is *inerrant.*
This is surely puzzling: I think I am an evangelical
Christian, but am I?

I can affirm, as I did at my ordination to the ministry
in 1965, that the Bible is "the only infallible rule of
faith and practice." By that I simply mean that I find
the Bible entirely trustworthy on matters of faith and
practice. This is not to say that I understand everything
the Bible teaches on matters of faith and practice. I
freely admit that there are many questions I cannot
answer even to my own satisfaction. For example, I do
not claim to know how to reconcile Paul's teachings on
election with the Bible's apparent commitment to the
notion that people are free and morally responsible
agents. Nor do I claim to know how to reconcile Paul's
statement that "there is neither male nor female . . .
in Christ" (Gal. 3:28) with some of his apparently
sexist teachings. But despite these problem areas, I can
and do believe that the Bible is the only infallible rule

of faith and practice. In matters of faith and practice it does not mislead us.

But the specific highly technical claim that the Bible is inerrant is one that in all humility I cannot affirm. Let us say that a book is "inerrant" if and only if it makes no false or misleading statements. Thus, to claim that the Bible is inerrant is to claim much more than that it is "the only infallible rule of faith and practice." It is to claim that the Bible contains *no errors at all*—none in history, geography, botany, astronomy, sociology, psychiatry, economics, geology, logic, mathematics, or any area whatsoever.

It is true that in most contexts of English usage the terms "infallible" and "inerrant" are synonymous. Nevertheless I believe that each term has come to have its own distinctive theological connotation. The word "infallible" appears in the Westminster Confession of Faith, a Reformed creedal statement of 1647 that has had enormous influence on subsequent evangelical theology. To many persons the term "infallible" seems to connote the notion that the Bible is entirely trustworthy on matters of faith and practice. What the Confession says is that all sixty-six books of the Bible "are given by inspiration of God, to be the rule of faith and life." It affirms what it calls the "entire perfection" and "infallible truth" of Scripture, but it seems to limit this to the Bible's role as a "rule of faith and life." (*The Book of Confessions,* Secs. 6.001–6.010, General Assembly of The United Presbyterian Church U.S.A., 1967.)

The word "inerrant" is a technical theological term used almost nowhere else but in the context of theological debates about the Bible. It seems to connote the notion that the Bible is entirely trustworthy on *all* matters. Accordingly, I will use the two terms in these senses in this book.

There are many evangelicals who believe in inerrancy, and some who hold inerrancy to be crucial to the evangelical Christian position. Some even go so far as to claim that a person cannot be considered evangelical unless he believes that the Bible is inerrant. I cannot agree with this. I consider myself an evangelical Christian and yet I do not affirm inerrancy. I do believe most, and perhaps all, of the doctrines typically held by evangelicals: the creation of the world by God; the fact that we are lost in sin and need divine redemption; the virgin birth of Christ; the substitutionary death of Christ on the cross; the divinity, bodily resurrection, and second coming of Christ; the need for persons to commit their lives in faith to Christ; etc.

Thus the puzzle: Am I an evangelical or not? How do we decide who is an evangelical and who is not? Must a person believe in inerrancy to be an evangelical? Is the claim that the Bible is inerrant true?

This last question provides the focus for this book. What I wish to do primarily is to examine the arguments that are typically given in support of the claim that the Bible is inerrant, and defend my own attitude toward the Bible. In Chapter 1, I will attempt to define the term "inerrant" with precision and care. I will examine as fairly as I can the theories of two contemporary defenders of the doctrine. Three major arguments emerge in the thought of those who advocate inerrancy. They are:

1. The Bible itself claims to be inerrant.

2. If the Bible is not inerrant, we have no sure word from God.

3. Anyone who denies inerrancy will end up denying other evangelical doctrines.

I will call the first "the Biblical argument," and I will discuss it in Chapter 2. I will call the second "the epistemological argument." It comes in many forms, and I will attempt to unravel and evaluate them in Chapter 3. And I will call the third "the slippery slide argument." This argument is difficult to understand precisely, but I will attempt to examine each of its possible interpretations in Chapter 4. In Chapter 5, I will offer some criticisms of inerrancy; in Chapter 6, I will summarize and defend my own attitude toward the Bible; and in Chapter 7, I will speak of some of the practical implications of inerrancy and alternative views of the Bible.

Frankly, I write this book with some misgivings. For one thing, one of my fears about the current intramural debate over inerrancy is that it will divide evangelicals into two hostile camps. I have no wish to contribute to any hostility or division. On the contrary, my intention in writing this book is precisely the opposite: I simply want inerrantists to understand the logic of the position of those evangelicals who do not affirm inerrancy, and I wish to argue that there is no reason on this issue to exclude anyone from the camp. Obviously I have no political quarrel with those who believe in inerrancy. I have no wish to exclude them from any camp, nor have I any hope that this book will change their minds. I only wish to help them understand my beliefs and those of others like me who are troubled and puzzled by the gauntlets that have been thrown down before us in recent months. I am thinking here of the strong statements that have been made by, among others, Francis Schaeffer and Harold Lindsell.

The other reason for misgivings on my part is that I am a philosopher, not a Biblical scholar. I have always felt that inerrancy is primarily an issue to be debated by Biblical scholars, but perhaps this is not true. Two of the three major arguments for inerrancy —the epistemological argument and the slippery slide argument—are essentially philosophical or apologetic arguments. Perhaps a philosopher can shed some light on them. The Biblical argument is obviously more exegetical than philosophical, but I will attempt to say some helpful things about it too.

Despite the misgivings, I feel a real need to write this book. Aside from the reasons already given, I find one truly compelling. I once knew a young evangelical Christian who at one point in his academic career decided that he could no longer affirm that the Bible is inerrant. Because of the heavy emphasis on inerrancy in the evangelical circles in which he had been raised, he took this to mean that he was no longer evangelical. In my opinion he was at this point still an evangelical, orthodox in his Christology and in other crucial areas. He might have been of real service to the evangelical Christian cause. The slippery slide argument can be something of a self-fulfilling prophecy. Tell a person that he descends to liberal Christianity once he gives up inerrancy and perhaps he will. I write this book with this young man and others like him in mind. If I can convince one such person to retain his evangelical Christian ties, life-style, and theology

despite his inability to affirm that the Bible is inerrant, then this work will have been worth the effort
and the risk.

This book—which could have been entitled
"Evangelicals and Inerrancy"—was written primarily with laypersons, college and seminary students,
and other nonexperts in theology and philosophy in
mind. I hope that what I have written is sufficiently
scholarly and illuminating to please the experts, but
I have attempted to produce a book that any intelli-
gent person can understand. I have tried to avoid
theological jargon. I have abstained from using the
symbols that philosophers usually find handy.
Where technical theological and philosophical terms
have had to be introduced I have tried to provide
convenient definitions. I have avoided using Greek
or Hebrew expressions. Since in my opinion con-
ciseness is a virtue, I am happy that this has turned
out to be a short book.

I would like to make it clear at the outset that I hold
to a high view of the Bible. I affirm that it is inspired,
authoritative, trustworthy, and, as I define the term,
infallible. I wish to emphasize this point so that there
will be no confusion as to my position. Also, I want to
affirm that my aim in this book is constructive rather
than destructive. I will criticize inerrancy, but my purpose is to strengthen—not weaken—the evangelical
Christian cause by making a clear and, I hope, convincing case for an evangelical attitude toward the Bible
that does not involve inerrancy. The "all or nothing"
arguments of many defenders of inerrancy give the
impression that there is no middle ground between

inerrancy, on the one hand, and neo-orthodox, liberal, or even atheistic attitudes toward the Bible, on the other. I want to show that there is another alternative, one that is both intellectually tenable and theologically acceptable to evangelicals.

As a token of my desire to unite rather than to divide, I have asked Clark Pinnock of Regent College, a noted defender of inerrancy, to write the Foreword. As well as for his kindness in contributing to the book in this way, I would also like to thank him for his valuable suggestions and criticisms. I also wish to thank my former teacher Daniel P. Fuller, who read an early draft of the manuscript and offered many helpful comments for which I am grateful, and my good friend and colleague Dr. Don Williams, an outstanding United Presbyterian evangelical, who gave detailed comments and suggestions. I also wish to mention several of my students and former students who helped in various ways, especially Greg Read, who allowed me to borrow from the extensive literature he has collected on inerrancy, and Dwight Mendoza and John Tannenbaum, who read and commented on the manuscript.

I would also like to note that Professor George Mavrodes read a version of Chapter 4 and saved me from making a logical error. A special word of thanks is due Pat Gayler, the secretary of the philosophy department at Claremont Men's College, for her usual accurate and faithful job of typing the manuscript. I wish also to mention my friend and neighbor Mark Branson, an outstanding worker in college ministry, for his encouragement and suggestions. Most of all, my wife, Charis, whose interest in this work was a great encouragement to me, made many suggestions that have improved it.

Despite the help of all these friends, I alone am responsible for this work, and any errors or deficiencies are to be attributed only to me.

S.T.D.

Claremont, California

I

INERRANCY

MY AIM IN THIS CHAPTER is to clarify as much as possible the doctrine that the Bible is inerrant. This is no easy task, for the doctrine comes in various forms, some of which are more elusive than others. It is important to state precisely my definitions of the primary concepts. The Bible is *inerrant* if and only if it makes no false or misleading statements on any topic whatsoever. The Bible is infallible if and only if it makes no false or misleading statements on any matter of faith and practice. In these senses, I personally hold that the Bible is infallible but not inerrant.

But what do the people who advocate inerrancy mean by this term? This is not easy to say, because there are various inerrancy doctrines in the air at the moment. Some people, for example, start with an exceedingly strong definition of the term, not unlike my definition above. But then in the light of the phenomenological difficulties that they find in the text of the Bible itself, they so qualify this notion that its original meaning seems to have disappeared.

I will not at this point undertake an investigation of the many theories of Biblical inerrancy that have been suggested. There are two things I want to do in this chapter: first, to list the various ways in which something like the strong notion of inerrancy defined above is typically qualified by defenders of inerrancy; and second, to look at the theories of two contemporary defenders of inerrancy.

Before I do so, let me point out a detail that must first be understood. Two sorts of possible "errors" in the Bible should be distinguished. The first are those which make purported false or misleading factual claims (e.g., it would be a factual error if the Bible somewhere said, "Egypt is north of Syria"). The second are those which occur where two or more accounts of the same event or fact are purportedly inconsistent (e.g., it would be inconsistent if one Gospel claimed that Jesus had a beard at the time of his crucifixion and another Gospel claimed that he was clean-shaven at the time of his crucifixion). In this second case, we would not know which text was mistaken, but at least one would have to be.

Let us now list the ways in which defenders of the doctrine of inerrancy qualify their position.

1. One point on which there is unanimity is that grammatical errors and other errors in form do not count as violations of the claim that the Bible is inerrant. This is important, because some Biblical books do contain grammatical solecisms—Mark, II Peter, and Revelation are examples. But inerrancy is almost always defined as I have defined it—that the Bible makes no false or misleading statements.

2. There is unanimity among present-day defenders of inerrancy on a second point as well: that inerrancy refers not to presently existing Bibles but to the *autographs.* That is, what is claimed to be inerrant is not the

King James Version or the Revised Standard Version of the Bible but the original texts of the Bible, the first copies of the various Biblical books.

This distinction has been ridiculed by some non-evangelical scholars, and it does seem to leave a permanently open door of escape for the advocate of inerrancy. No matter how clearly a given passage is in error, he can always evade the issue and retain his notion of inerrancy by saying: "Yes, but this is an error of transmission. It was not present in the autograph." Since no Biblical autographs have survived, there is no way to refute this claim. This move does seem intellectually dishonest, especially if there is no textual evidence that the alleged error is indeed due to a transmission problem.

However, this argument is in fact seldom used by sophisticated defenders of inerrancy, and for good reason. The science of textual criticism has advanced to the point where we know very well what the autographs said in the case of the vast majority of Biblical texts. Some textual problems remain, of course, where we are not sure among several variant readings what the autograph actually said. But these problems are few indeed in relation to the whole Bible, and no crucial point of fact or doctrine seems to hinge upon them.

3. A third qualification often made is that to constitute an actual falsification of the claim that the Bible is inerrant, the Biblical author's *intended meaning* must be shown to be false or misleading. This sort of move is perhaps not totally unacceptable, but stated in this simple way it is surely not helpful. For example, in Matt. 13:31–32 Jesus says that the "mustard seed

. . . is the smallest of all seeds." This does not happen to be true: botanists know of smaller seeds than the mustard seed. So one obvious way to avoid the claim that this is an error in Scripture is to deny that it was Jesus' intent to make a point about botany. But there is a difficulty here. Surely Jesus did not make his statement about the mustard seed *unintentionally,* i.e., as if it just inadvertently "slipped out" like, say, a Freudian slip. Thus instead of speaking simply about what the Biblical author *intended to say* (surely Jesus did indeed intend to say that the "mustard seed . . . is the smallest of all seeds"), it might be better to speak of *the main point he was making.* In context, the main point, that Jesus was making in Matt. 13:31–32 clearly has nothing to do with botany but rather with the nature of the Kingdom of Heaven. If so, the "intent" qualification on inerrancy should now say something to this effect: The Bible can be shown to be errant only if the main point being made in some Biblical text is false or misleading.

But even if we make this change, two difficulties remain. First, in a great many passages there is room for debate over what constitutes the main point being made. This too seems to present the defender of inerrancy with a perennially open door of escape. His intellectual honesty will depend on whether or not his exegetical efforts are illicitly influenced by these sorts of apologetic considerations. Second, we might wonder about the aptness of even the amended qualification. Of course nothing prevents a theologian from defining "inerrant" in any way that pleases him and from claiming that the Bible, *in his sense,* is indeed inerrant. But suppose a friend communicates to me a true point and in the process says something false or misleading. Perhaps he is trying to convince me that Picasso was a great artist (which is true), but as evidence for this claim he points out the greatness of a painting that he thinks is a Picasso but is actually a Klee. I would regard this as overwhelming evidence that my friend is not inerrant, despite the fact that his main point is true. Could not the same thing be said about the Bible—even if all the errors we can find are different from the main points being made in the passages in which they occur?

The two final qualifications I will mention are listed by Archibald Alexander Hodge and Benjamin B. Warfield.[1] They are:

4. A genuine contradiction does not exist simply because the same event or fact is recorded in two different ways. What must be shown is that the parallel passages are incapable of harmonization with each other.

5. To constitute a genuine error, the mistake or contradiction in question must be indisputably false or indisputably contradictory. It cannot be just a difficulty that may later be resolved.

If at times there seems to be a strange air of unreality about debates over Biblical inerrancy, we can now see some reasons why. When we list all our qualifications, it appears that a purported error in the text will actually falsify the claim that the Bible is inerrant if and only if:

1. The purported error concerns a Biblical claim rather than Biblical grammar;

2. The purported error occurs in the autograph;

3. The purported error concerns the main point being made in the passage where it occurs;

   and either

4. The purported error is an inconsistency that can be shown to be incapable of harmonization;

   or

5. The purported error is indisputably false and not just a resolvable difficulty.

No doubt not all these conditions would be accepted by all defenders of inerrancy; and perhaps some defenders of inerrancy would list other conditions not mentioned here. But this is certainly enough to show how difficult it is to say precisely what is meant by the apparently simple claim that the Bible is inerrant.

The air of unreality that often pervades the discussion is perhaps a product of two factors. First, if all or even most of the above qualifications are accepted, the doctrine that the Bible is inerrant clearly becomes unfalsifiable. It is hard to see how *any* purported error could pass all the tests. For example, historical and geographical errors can be excluded on condition 3; internal inconsistencies in two or more Biblical texts can be excluded on condition 4; and, indeed, any imaginable purported error can be excluded on condition 2 or 5. In fairness I should note that some defenders of inerrancy are quite prepared to admit that there are phenomenological difficulties in the Bible that they cannot resolve. But it is still true that condition

4 or 5 is also typically invoked, so that the difficulties do not constitute falsifications of the claim that the Bible is inerrant.

In the second place, those who qualify inerrancy in at least some of the above ways argue quite vociferously against alternative views of the Bible. But it is difficult to spell out the precise differences between inerrancy, thus defined and qualified, and infallibility as I have defined it; or "limited inerrancy," a term preferred—and used pejoratively—by advocates of "full inerrancy."

One other point should be mentioned. Those who posit inerrancy obviously do so as a means of defending the Bible and making the strongest possible case for its inspiration and authority. But if inerrancy is defined in terms of freedom from factual error, we might wonder whether this doctrine says *enough* about the Bible. For the Bible does a great deal more than make factual claims. This is true even if we broaden the scope of the term "factual claim" to include theological and moral statements. In fact, one of the most obvious characteristics of the Bible is the great diversity of literary forms we find in it: history, law, biography, theology, ethics, poetry, liturgy, letters, wise sayings, sermons, stories, parables, allegories, apocalyptic literature, etc. In addition, figurative language, Oriental hyperbole, and other forms of expression that differ from simple declarative statements abound in the Bible. It is difficult to see how *inerrancy,* as it is usually understood, is even relevant to many of these forms. For example, consider the following sentences from the Bible:

You shall not bear false witness against your neighbor.
(Ex. 20:16)

> Make a joyful noise to the LORD, all the
>   lands!
> Serve the LORD with gladness!
> Come into his presence with singing!
>   (Ps. 100:1–2)

Perhaps the defender of inerrancy can expand his notion of "inerrant" to show how these sentences are
inerrant, but it is not clear at this point how they can
be so.

As a way of illustrating some of the difficulties I have
listed, I wish now to look at the notion of Biblical
inerrancy as defended by two contemporary evangelicals, Harold Lindsell[2] and Daniel P. Fuller.[3] They are
not the only contemporary advocates of inerrancy, but
their views are perhaps representative of the notions
of "full" and "limited" inerrancy respectively, and the
difficulties each faces are instructive for our purposes.

LINDSELL'S VIEW OF FULL INERRANCY

Lindsell believes that inerrancy is the most important theological issue of our period. In his recent book,
The Battle for the Bible, he has written a militant and
vigorous defense of the doctrine. Belief in inerrancy,
he says, is a watershed: those who hold the doctrine
are true evangelicals and those who do not are not. It
is little wonder he feels this strongly, for Lindsell believes that denial of inerrancy leads to denial of other
evangelical doctrines, and to doom for any denomina-
tion, seminary, or Christian organization. Denial of

inerrancy inevitably leads to such ills as loss of missionary outreach and interest in evangelism, to spiritual
sloth and decay, and finally to apostasy.[4]

Lindsell would reject my earlier distinction between
"infallible" and "inerrant": he believes the two terms
are synonymous. He defines an error as "a mis-state-
ment or something that is contrary to fact." And in
claiming that the Bible is inerrant, he means that "it
is not false, mistaken, or defective."[5] The Bible, he
says,

> can be trusted as truthful in all its parts. It communi-
> cates religious truth, not religious error. But there is
> more. Whatever it communicates is to be trusted and
> can be relied upon as being true. The Bible is not a
> textbook on chemistry, astronomy, philosophy, or
> medicine. But when it speaks on matters having to do
> with these or any other subjects, the Bible does not lie
> to us. It does not contain error of any kind.[6]

This is an exceedingly strong view of the trustworthiness of the Bible, but as we will see, Lindsell illustrates
my point that advocates of inerrancy often qualify
their strong commitment to the doctrine in important
ways.

In *The Battle for the Bible* there are four major arguments for inerrancy. The first is the Biblical argument.
Lindsell argues that the Bible teaches that it is inerrant
—or at least that it teaches that it is inspired; and he
argues further that it cannot truly be inspired unless it
is also inerrant.[7] The second is what might be called
the historical argument. It is that with a few exceptions
inerrancy, as defined by Lindsell, has been held by
theologians throughout the history of the church and

is therefore not a new doctrine invented by modern
fundamentalists, as some liberal scholars charge.[8] The
third is the epistemological argument[9] and the fourth
is the slippery slide argument.[10] Lindsell makes liberal
use of both arguments, but I will defer comment on
them until later.

Three of Lindsell's arguments are not peculiar to
him, for nearly every defender of inerrancy makes use
of them. Since I will devote a chapter to each of these
in turn, I shall not discuss them here. His second argument, the historical argument, is in a way his own. I
will leave its in-depth examination to those who are
more qualified. I will, however, record a reservation
about it. While high views of inspiration and authority
have indeed nearly always been held, Lindsell's insis-
tence that his own notion of *inerrancy* has nearly always
been held is, in my opinion, highly questionable. His
case is based on a particularly selective use of quotations, at least in some instances. For example, Calvin's
fairly cavalier attitude toward minor difficulties in the
Bible and Luther's negative attitude toward the Epistle
of James and other New Testament books are not
considered seriously.

Lindsell is quite vocal in his rejection of "limited
inerrancy"—which would roughly correspond to what
I call "infallibility," the doctrine that there are topics
on which the Bible is not inerrant.[11] This is consistent
with his extremely strong definition of "inerrant."
Nevertheless, Lindsell himself qualifies his strong notion of inerrancy in important ways, some of which are
understandable and some of which are puzzling. For
example, it is understandable when he holds that only
factual and not grammatical errors count as violations

of the claim that the Bible is inerrant; and when he holds that inerrancy is a claim about the autographs, not about presently existing Bibles.[12]

But two other qualifications are surprising, given Lindsell's claim that the Bible "does not contain error of any kind." They come up in his discussion of the phenomena of Scripture. The first is that in response to the numerical discrepancies occasionally found in the Bible—e.g., the "missing thousand" discrepancy between Num. 25:9 and I Cor. 10:8—Lindsell endorses the view that inerrancy relates only to the standards of accuracy that were prevalent at the time of the writing of the text. Standards were less rigorous then, Lindsell appears to be saying. If the correct number of people who died in the Shittim plague were, say, 23,-500, then both Paul and the writer of Numbers can be correct. "It would be both easy and correct for one to use the 24,000 figure and the other the 23,000 figure, since both were speaking in round numbers."[13] Of course Lindsell can qualify his notion of inerrancy in any way he pleases, but I do not see how he can take this approach to the "missing thousand" discrepancy and still claim that the Bible "does not contain error *of any kind*" (italics mine). Surely an error *of some kind* has been made either in Numbers or in I Corinthians.

The second is that in response to the mustard seed problem, and in other contexts, Lindsell limits inerrancy to the *intent* of the Biblical writer, although he seems to do it rather halfheartedly.[14] Again, Lindsell is free to qualify his notion of inerrancy in any way he pleases, but one wonders, in the light of his strong definition of the term, whether inerrancy is a doctrine about what the Bible says or about what the Biblical writer intends to say. For it is surely the notion of *intent* that allows Fuller and other advocates of "limited inerrancy" to say that Scripture is *both* inerrant *and* liable to error on historical, scientific, and other matters. They say the Bible does not intend to teach on these subjects. However, the notion that the Bible can be mistaken in science, history, or any other area is one that Lindsell most clearly will not countenance.

It is in relation to the phenomenological difficulties actually found in the Bible that Lindsell's notion of inerrancy is subject to the most strains.[15] He deals with the phenomena of Scripture in Ch. 9, entitled "Discrepancies in Scripture," and as one would expect, he attempts to show that all alleged errors or contradictions in the Bible can be explained or harmonized and that they do not therefore disprove inerrancy. "Apparent discrepancies," he says, "are no more than that."[16] His handling of several alleged discrepancies can be questioned, but one point that shows clearly the grotesque extremes to which advocates of inerrancy must occasionally go is his handling of the problem of Peter's denial.[17]

As is well known, Matt. 26:34, 74–75; Luke 22:34, 60–61; and John 13:38; 18:27 have Jesus telling Peter that he will deny him three times before the cock crows, and they record that this is exactly what later happened. But the difficulty is that Mark 14:30, 72 has Jesus telling Peter that he will deny him three times before the cock crows *twice,* and Mark records that this is exactly what later happened. How many times did the cock actually crow? It appears that our sources are inconsistent. We cannot know what actually occurred. All we know is that *either* Mark or the Matthew-Luke-

John account is mistaken—they cannot both be correct —and thus the Bible is not inerrant. Lindsell's response to this, following J. M. Cheney, is a rather intricate and ingenious weaving together of the accounts of Peter's denial from all four Gospels. This results, he says, in one consistent narrative and no errors. It turns out, he claims, that Peter denied Jesus not three but *six* times and that the cock crowed twice —once after the third denial and once after the sixth.

It is obvious that serious difficulties abound in the Cheney-Lindsell proposal, and Lindsell does not appear to have noticed them. I will mention three. Perhaps it is unfair to criticize Lindsell for his failure to make use of source and form criticism as they illuminate the story of Peter's denial, for he makes it clear in *The Battle for the Bible* that he has no sympathy for Biblical criticism. I do not believe this is a proper attitude for evangelicals to take. We must embrace the historical-critical study of the Bible even if we question the assumptions and conclusions of some of the critics, but I do not wish to argue this point here.

1. There are internal difficulties in the scheme. For example, Mark 14:72 ("And Peter remembered how Jesus had said to him, 'Before the cock crows twice, you will deny me three times' "), which Lindsell places after the sixth denial, is by the logic of his own account in error. It should say "six times" rather than "three times."

2. Lindsell quite freely rearranges the order of the denials as found in the Gospels. For example, he has Mark's "maid of the high priest" eliciting Peter's *third*

denial, while Mark has her eliciting his *first*. This violates not only Mark's order but Matthew's and Luke's
as well, for they follow Mark at this point. There are
other instances of Lindsell's reordering the events of
the denial as recorded by the Evangelists—which is
puzzling in one who has such a high regard for the text
as Lindsell claims to have.

3. The Lindsell-Cheney proposal differs in important ways from the account of each of the four Gospels
taken singly. The plain teaching of all four Evangelists
is that the cock crowed after three denials and there
were no subsequent denials. It is also the plain teaching of all three Synoptic Gospels that after three denials and the crowing of the cock Peter broke down. The
Fourth Gospel does not dispute this. Lindsell's elaborate account denies both of these facts. Furthermore,
the accounts of the Evangelists have about them a
psychological ring of truth that Lindsell's rearrange-
ment lacks. Why didn't Peter break down after the
third denial and the first crowing of the cock and not
until after the sixth and the second? It takes audacity
to claim that there were six denials when *all four* Gospels record only three. It would be interesting to hear
Lindsell's conjecture as to why each Gospel records
three instead of the claimed six. It would be equally
interesting to hear why "three" instead of the claimed
"six" in each Gospel is not at least *some* kind of error.

So Lindsell's attempt to salvage inerrancy in the face
of these difficulties is an elaborate failure. Of course,
for someone who accepts inerrancy *a priori* and who
must therefore make the text conform to this notion,

such machinations as these are understandable. But other and perhaps equally attractive alternatives beckon for the advocate of inerrancy. Since the accounts of Matthew and Luke seem here to be based on a common tradition, why not have three sets of three denials—one for Mark, one for John, and one for Matthew-Luke? Or why not just deny *a priori* that the word "twice" in Mark 14:30 and the words "a second time" and "twice" in Mark 14:72 are in the autograph of Mark? Why not just attribute them to a later scribal error? Or better yet, why not reclassify the whole problem, calling it a "difficulty" that will one day be resolved rather than a "contradiction"?[18]

Certainly there are serious problems with these alternatives too. The first is open to the same criticisms as is Lindsell's scheme, the second has no textual evidence to support it, and the third is intellectually dishonest. There is, of course, a much simpler alternative than any of these, but Lindsell is unwilling to consider it: Mark's account (on this one point) is simply inconsistent with the accounts of the other Gospels.

FULLER'S VIEW OF LIMITED INERRANCY

Daniel P. Fuller's theory of Biblical inerrancy is to be found primarily in his two brief articles "Benjamin B. Warfield's View of Faith and History" and "The Nature of Biblical Inerrancy." As we might expect, given only about thirteen total pages of exposition, his theory is incomplete and raises many questions. It is easily misunderstood, and has been criticized. I will argue that some of the criticisms that have been made are not justified. Although I cannot accept Fuller's position, it is closer to my own than Lindsell's. In addition, his arguments are much more closely reasoned, scholarly, and calm than Lindsell's.

Fuller is quite prepared to say that the Bible is inerrant, but he does not mean the same thing by this that Lindsell does. In order to understand what he means we must ask what an "error" is. Errors, or at least the sorts of errors that are relevant to the notion of Biblical inerrancy, are, he says, relative to intention: "A communication can be in error only if it fails to live up to the intention of its author." A doctor might tell his patient a true principle of healthful living but in an illustration of it commit a factual error. But suppose his intention was merely to illustrate his true principle; and suppose his illustration *does* illustrate it well. Then, says Fuller, he has not erred. This applies not only to persons but to books. "A book is inerrant only against the criterion of its writer's intention. Interpretation is not concerned with everything that was in an author's mind, but only with the meaning which he necessarily implied by what he intended to say."[19]

Thus, in order to know whether or not the Bible is inerrant we must know its overall purpose, or the intention of God, who inspired it. Following II Tim. 3:15, Fuller thinks he knows the purpose of the Bible: it is to make us "wise unto salvation" (KJV). The Bible's purpose is not to make us wise unto botany or psychology or geology or history. Rather, it is to impart God's revelation, to set forth revelational truths by recounting and explaining the meaning of God's mighty acts in history. He says, "The Biblical writers make it clear that their purpose was to report the happenings and meanings of the redemptive acts of God in history so that men might be made wise unto salvation."[20]

By this criterion, the Bible is inerrant. It perfectly lives up to its intention; it does indeed recount and explain the correct meaning of God's redemptive acts in history; and it does so "in the most pedagogically suitable manner for the original hearers and readers." Thus the Bible is not just a record and an explanation of God's past revelations of himself in history: it is itself a revelation. Indeed, the whole Bible is revelatory.[21] It is in this sense that Fuller defends inerrancy. He is saying that the entire Bible, "in the whole and in the part," is inerrant in that it never fails to fulfill its purpose of making the reader wise unto salvation. Fuller may on this basis resist being called a defender of "limited inerrancy"; I apply the term to him because (in opposition to people like Lindsell) he admits that there may be other criteria under whose influence it would be appropriate to say that the Bible errs.

Indeed, Fuller admits that there are certain things in the Bible that are only incidentally related to fulfilling its intention of accounting and interpreting God's redemptive acts. These he calls "non-revelational matters"—e.g., Biblical statements on such topics as geology, meteorology, cosmology, botany, astronomy, geography, etc. Here, he admits, the Bible is fallible. Since its aim is not to teach truths on such topics as these, it is still by his earlier criterion inerrant. Where the Bible is inerrant is on intentional matters, things it intends to teach. These are what Fuller calls "revelational matters." Some have criticized Fuller here, claiming that he provides no criterion for distinguishing revelational (intentional) from nonrevelational (nonintentional) matters in the Bible. But I believe this is unfair. Fuller does indeed provide a fairly useful criterion. Revelational matters are Biblical claims that cannot be tested, that is, verified or falsified by human beings—e.g., "God created the heavens and the earth," "Christ died for our sins." These are truths concerning "what eye cannot see nor ear can hear by itself." Nonrevelational matters (e.g., "Jesus died on the cross," "the mustard seed is the smallest of all seeds") are "capable of being checked out by human investigation, i.e., knowable by what eye can see or ear can hear."[22]

Fuller is aware that the defender of full inerrancy will insist that the Bible's statements in these areas be true as well. But this view, he claims, ends up tacitly denying that the Bible is grounded in history. It forces people to exegetical extremes where the Bible is not interpreted historically. For example, he criticizes Edward J. Young, who refuses to accept what Fuller regards as the historically acceptable explanation of the problem of reconciling Gen. 11:26 to 12:4 with Acts 7:1–4. (The problem is that Stephen's speech in Acts says that Abraham left Haran only after his father, Terah, died, while the Genesis texts imply that Terah lived for many years after Abraham's departure from Haran.) Fuller says Young will not do so because it would violate his commitment to full inerrancy, i.e., inerrancy on nonrevelational as well as revelational matters. This touches upon one of Fuller's deepest concerns: his commitment to an *inductive* rather than a deductive approach to the Bible. The deductivist begins with a theological presupposition or *a priori* (e.g., full inerrancy) and then must make everything in the Bible conform to it. If he rejects probable historical explanations because they violate his *a priori,* he is, says Fuller, in effect disallowing the use of historical arguments in support of other more crucial Christian claims, e.g., the resurrection or the even larger claim that God works in history.[23]

Induction, for Fuller, means willingness to let historical evidence guide one throughout one's investigation of Scripture. The Bible, he says, must "always be subject to historical investigation without any theological *a prioris.*"[24] How, then, does Fuller come to his conclusion that the Bible is inerrant? Fuller claims to follow Warfield here: he begins with an open-minded historical (inductive) look at the Bible and there discovers certain signs ("indicia") of the Bible's reliability. Quoting the Westminster Confession of Faith (Ch. I, Sec. 5), he notes some of the indicia:[25]

> . . . the heavenliness of the matter, the efficacy of the doctrine, the majesty of the style, the consent of all the parts, the scope of the whole (which is to give all glory to God), the full discovery it makes of the only way of man's salvation.

The indicia convince us that the Bible is the word of God. From there, Fuller says, we move to an investigation of what the Bible says about itself, and there we discover that the Bible claims to be verbally inspired, authoritative, and inerrant. That is, the indicia inductively convince us of the truth of what the Bible says about itself, and an inductive study of the Bible shows that the Bible itself claims to be inerrant on revelational matters.[26]

Fuller has been criticized here on a logical point.

Some take him to be cheating. They interpret him as saying that the Bible is inerrant only when its statements are revelational and thus nontestable, and that any Biblical statement that is falsified will immediately be classified by him as nonrevelational, enabling him to continue to hold that the Bible is, in his sense, inerrant.[27] This is a possible interpretation of Fuller's published words which a more complete expression of his views might have avoided, but I believe it is untrue to his intended meaning. He is not saying that the Bible cannot err on revelational matters and that it can on nonrevelational matters. He is saying that on nonrevelational matters there may be errors in Scripture, but that on revelational matters (i.e., on what the Bible intentionally teaches) he has discovered none yet and hopes he never will. He will allow induction to guide him even here, despite his clear belief that a discovered error on a revelational matter makes the whole Bible questionable. In response to Pinnock he says: "I sincerely hope that as I continue my historical-grammatical exegesis of Scripture, I shall find no error in its teachings. But I can only affirm inerrancy with high probability."[28]

One last point in the exposition of Fuller's position should be mentioned. It might be asked of Fuller why God allows the Bible to contain errors on nonrevelational matters (such as the claim that the mustard seed is the smallest of all seeds). Fuller's answer is *accommodation.* In verbally inspiring the Biblical writers, God had to accommodate himself to the ignorance of the people who would read the Bible—otherwise he would not have been able to communicate with us. Thus, Fuller says, "the Biblical writers were also supernaturally enabled by God to understand the best way to take certain non-revelational, cultural matters, and without changing them, use them to enhance the communication of revelational truths to the original hearers or readers."[29]

Thus Fuller insists that inerrancy, properly understood, allows and even requires that the Holy Spirit leave unchanged nonrevelational, culturally conditioned statements that are technically in error. If Jesus' hearers erroneously believed that the mustard seed is the smallest of all seeds, then it would have hindered Jesus' attempt to convey a revelational point in Matt. 13:32 had he omnisciently referred by name to whatever seed *is* smallest. If Stephen's hearers erroneously believed that Abraham left Haran only after Terah died, it would have ruined the revelational point that Stephen ("full of the Holy Spirit," Acts 7:55) was attempting to make had he corrected this belief. In order to communicate to beings whose knowledge is limited, God must accommodate himself to their ignorance. Communication is impossible apart from words that are understandable in the cultural and historical situation of the hearer.

FULLER'S POSITION CRITICIZED

Fuller's theory has been criticized by fellow evangelicals, and I too will raise some objections. However, there are several points where I agree with Fuller. For example, I agree with his commitment to the inductive method and his willingness to expose all parts of his theory to historical reasoning. Thus I too will only claim to have a high degree of probability

rather than deductive certainty that the Bible is infallible. I also agree with Fuller that the Bible contains
historical and scientific errors. (I do not know that
Fuller ever explicitly says this, but I believe his theory
implies it.) And I agree that such errors have no serious theological or apologetic consequences.

But I would still wish to raise some questions about
Fuller's theory. Since Fuller admits to the possibility of
Biblical errors on nonrevelational matters, why does
he want to retain the term "inerrant" at all? Of course
he can define the term in any way he pleases, just as
I have given a technical definition for purposes of my
theory of the term "infallible." But it does seem odd
to claim that "a communication can be in error *only* if
it fails to live up to the intention of its author" (italics
mine). As a persuasive definition of the term "error,"
this fails to convince me. Surely there are other ways
than this that a communication can be in error. Even
if Fuller insists that we accept his definition, this will
hardly settle the dispute. For the believer in full inerrancy will then simply make Fuller a gift of the term
"inerrant," i.e., he will let Fuller use this term in any
way he pleases and simply make up a new term to
cover *his* concern. For example, he might now wonder
whether or not the Bible is "errorless"—and Fuller
will have to say no. This does not constitute much in
the way of a criticism of Fuller. It is just a way of
making the point that there is a real sense in which
Fuller does *not* believe in Biblical inerrancy, despite
his protests to the contrary. I suspect that Fuller would
agree with this.

Why is Fuller prepared to allow that the Bible can
err in nonrevelational matters? Clearly it is because of

his theory of accommodation. God must find the best way of communicating his revelation to finite human beings, and so he must accommodate himself to our ignorance and occasionally commit errors. It is easy to appreciate what Fuller is driving at. We would not understand God if he shared with us the fullness of his divine knowledge. And I myself recall once congratulating my five-year-old son, in the midst of a reading lesson, on his announcing that the word "bought" is spelled "bot." In order to make a point, I accommodated myself to his rudimentary knowledge of spelling and erroneously told him he had spelled the word correctly.

There appears to be a distinction here that ought to be made. The notion of accommodation seems able to *explain* why some errors are made, but it certainly does not seem to *demand* that errors be made. If the Bible, as Fuller claims, was verbally inspired by an omniscient and omnipotent being, one wonders why its accommodational errors could not have been entirely avoided. For example, why didn't Jesus merely say, "The mustard seed is a small seed"? Or why didn't he make his point without mentioning mustard seeds at all? In other words, Fuller's justification of accommodational errors in the Bible will work only if in each case there was available to the Biblical writer no equally good or better inerrant way to make his point. And this seems dubious.

The obvious question is: If accommodation allows for errors on nonrevelational matters, why not on revelational matters too? Surely we are ignorant in these areas as well—perhaps even more ignorant than we are on nonrevelational matters. Why doesn't the

Bible err here too? Fuller's reply to this, I believe, would be twofold. First, he holds that the passages in which the Bible speaks about its own reliability refer only to revelational matters, e.g., doctrine, reproof, correction, and instruction in righteousness (II Tim. 3:16). He says, "Let us observe that when the doctrinal verses [i.e., verses where the Bible speaks about itself] teach or imply inerrancy, it is always in connection with revelational knowledge, not in connection with knowledge which makes a man wise unto botany, meteorology, cosmology, or paleontology, i.e., knowledge which is non-revelational simply because it is readily accessible to men."[30] I will not dispute this point here. Suffice it to say that in order to make this claim stick, Fuller will have to answer both people like me, who believe that the Bible teaches its own inspiration, authority, and reliability but not any sort of inerrancy; and people like Lindsell, who believe that the Bible teaches full inerrancy.

Fuller's second reply would be what I call the epistemological argument. Since I will examine this argument in detail later, I will make only a brief comment here. Fuller is convinced that the truth of the whole Bible is destroyed if the Bible is ever found to err in revelational matters or in nonrevelational matters on which revelation depends. He says: "If there is one error anywhere in what Scripture intends to teach, then everything it intends to say is suspect and we have not even one sure word from God."[31] My comment is this: Actually, on Fuller's assumptions, we have no sure word from God unless we can surely (infallibly) distinguish revelational passages (where Fuller has yet to discover an error) from nonrevelational passages (where Scripture may err, but where it does not matter). Earlier I admitted that Fuller does provide a fairly useful criterion: A passage is nonrevelational if the truth of its claim is testable by humans. But in order to bear the weight that Fuller's version of the epistemological argument makes it carry, we seem to need much more than a rough-and-ready criterion: we seem to need an infallible criterion. Otherwise it might fail or we might misuse it and thus produce the melancholy result that we have not one sure word from God.

One final point. There seems to be an ambiguity in Fuller's argument between the *intention of the whole Bible* and the *intention of a particular Biblical writer in a particular passage.* It may be that Fuller is correct that the intention of the Bible is to make us "wise unto salvation," but it would be odd to claim that this is the purpose of every single passage in the Bible. For instance, why cannot the intent of the writer of Gen., ch. 5, be to give us a correct chronology of the descendants of Adam? No doubt there is revelational content here; sermons probably have been preached on Gen., ch. 5, but this does not appear to be the main intent of the passage.

Thus, contrary to what Fuller in places implies, there is no necessary connection between the revelational content of a passage and the main intention of the writer in writing it. Can it ever be a Biblical writer's intent to write a nonrevelational (empirically testable) proposition? Here Fuller seems to me to be unclear. He certainly seems in places to deny this. Speaking of the truth of the time spans in Gen., ch. 5, he says:

Since such matters, however, are non-revelational, they lie outside the boundary of the Biblical writer's intention, and are therefore irrelevant to the question of Biblical inerrancy.[32]

But this seems an arbitrary *a priori* assumption on Fuller's part that ought rightly to be rejected by him as noninductive. In other places, however, he recognizes that some revelational (intentional) matters in the Bible are historically verifiable or falsifiable—e.g., the resurrection.[33] Where a historically verifiable or falsifiable proposition is essential to revelation, recording it can indeed be the main intention of a Biblical writer. So there are places where Fuller will in the end have to insist on the inerrant status of humanly verifiable or falsifiable statements, which seems to contradict some of what he says in other places. I take this too to be an ambiguity in Fuller's position which a more complete exposition might have avoided. As for myself, I see no reason to deny that the main intent of Biblical writers in a great many passages is to record what Fuller calls nonrevelational facts, and I believe Gen., ch. 5, is one such place.

However, my main objection to Fuller, and indeed one of my major objections to nearly every defender of inerrancy, revolves around the very usefulness of the notion of *intention* as a device for solving disputes over Biblical inerrancy. I will deal with this matter in Chapter 5.

2

THE
BIBLICAL
ARGUMENT

THE FIRST MAJOR ARGUMENT for inerrancy is what
I will call "the Biblical argument." It comes in two
forms. The simple form is this: "The Bible claims to
be inerrant; therefore the Bible is inerrant." In its
more complex form it says: "The Bible claims to be
inspired by God, and a book cannot be inspired by
God unless it is inerrant; therefore, the Bible is inerrant." My primary aim in this chapter will be to see
whether or not these arguments are sound.

Before we proceed, there is a logical detail that
requires our attention. There is an apparent circularity
to the Biblical argument. In logical form, the simple
Biblical argument appears to run in this way:

1. The Bible claims to be inerrant.

2. Therefore, the Bible is inerrant.

Aside from the question of the truth of 1, this argument is obviously invalid, because 2 does not logically
follow from 1. The argument becomes formally valid
only when we add a third premise:

3. Whatever the Bible claims is true.

The new argument formed by 1, 3, and 2 does appear
to be formally valid: 1 and 3 do indeed entail 2. However, this argument is informally invalid since it quite
patently begs the question. Since 3 is simply an alternative way of stating 2, the argument smuggles its conclusion into the premises.

Does this vitiate the Biblical argument before it
even begins? In one sense, yes. The Biblical argument
appears to be totally useless as a device for convincing
someone *who does not already accept 3* to believe that the
Bible is inerrant. The Biblical argument simply cannot
do that job. To the person who does not accept 3 or
who has not made a policy decision to believe whatever the Bible says, the Biblical argument is virtually
worthless.

But this does not mean that the Biblical argument
has no usefulness at all in theology. For it may indeed
be a cogent argument for the person who accepts 3 or
who has made a policy decision to believe whatever
the Bible says. It does seem that this must include all
evangelical Christians, for one mark of evangelicals is
their commitment to the Bible as their standard and
source of doctrine. For such a person, it seems a perfectly acceptable procedure to wonder what the Bible
says about itself and then to adopt whatever view of
the Bible the person decides the Bible teaches. (For
example, "Smith says that Smith always tells the truth"
is not a good argument for Smith's veracity for someone who does not already believe that Smith always
tells the truth or who has not made a policy decision
to believe whatever Smith says. But to someone who
does or has, this may indeed be a good argument.)

Thus the Biblical argument is not entirely ruined by

the circularity it has in some contexts. In fact, the evangelical in a sense is *obligated* to inquire after and accept the Bible's view of itself. For the evangelical is one who commits himself to the policy of accepting a doctrine if and only if it is either explicitly taught in the Bible or else is presupposed or implied by what is explicitly taught in the Bible. If an evangelical rejects what he discovers to be the Bible's view of itself, he rejects the procedure by which any suggested doctrine is to be accepted or rejected. So the Biblical argument does appear to have some possible theological usefulness, at least for those who want to believe what the Bible teaches. What *actual* usefulness it has will depend on the truth of the proposition that the Bible claims to be inerrant. I will turn to this question now.

THE BIBLE DOES NOT CLAIM INERRANCY

Let me begin with a quotation from Everett F. Harrison:

> One must grant that the Bible itself, in advancing its own claim of inspiration, says nothing precise about inerrancy. This remains a conclusion to which devout minds have come because of the divine character of Scripture.[34]

I quite agree with Harrison. One will search in vain for a Biblical passage that teaches that the Bible is inerrant, that it is nowhere misleading or mistaken on any subject whatsoever. Defenders of inerrancy often do boldly claim that "the Bible teaches its own inerrancy,"[35] but this is not easy to understand. As we have seen, "inerrant" is a highly technical term that must be defined carefully and qualified in several ways before it is even relevant to the status of the Bible. It is difficult to see how such a notion could be taught in the Bible, a book that contains little systematic theology or apologetics. Its writers were not familiar with the reasons why later theologians would feel the need for a doctrine such as inerrancy. For obvious reasons they were not familiar with the phenomenological difficulties in the Bible that lead some to deny that it is inerrant. So it is not surprising that we find nowhere in the Bible the claim that the Bible is inerrant.

What the Bible does clearly teach, I believe, is its own inspiration, authority, and reliability. As we might expect, there is no systematic teaching in the Bible about itself. What we find are many unsystematic, scattered, but nearly unanimous comments on these three points. Let me now say a few things about each.

1. The Bible testifies to its own inspiration. The two classic statements on inspiration are found in II Tim. 3:15–16 and II Peter 1:20–21:

> From childhood you have been acquainted with the sacred writings which are able to instruct you for salvation through faith in Christ Jesus. All scripture is inspired by God and profitable for teaching, for reproof, for correction, and for training in righteousness.

> First of all you must understand this, that no prophecy of scripture is a matter of one's own interpretation, because no prophecy ever came by the impulse of man, but men moved by the Holy Spirit spoke from God.

The word that is translated "inspired" literally means "God-breathed," or "breathed out by God." Precisely how God "breathed out" Scripture is far from clear. We know too much about the history of the formation of the Bible to believe that it was, so to speak, dropped to us from heaven by parachute. The books of the Bible were written by human authors whose theological concerns, historical and cultural settings, and idiosyncracies of style influenced their writing. This seems to rule out any dictation theory of inspiration, whereby God "breathed out" the Scriptures directly and the human authors simply acted as tape recorders, passively repeating what God breathed. Somehow, then, inspiration must involve both God and human beings as instruments. This seems to be what the passage in II Peter says: "men moved by the Holy Spirit" wrote the Scriptures.

Precisely how this worked is obviously a mystery, and the Bible gives no clear teaching on it. Because of this, theories of inspiration usually arise under the influence of the theorist's opinion of the authority and reliability that the Bible has or must have. Thus inerrantists typically come up with a notion of inspiration such that "Book x is inspired" entails "Book x is inerrant." I do not believe in inerrancy, and so my notion of inspiration does not involve inerrancy. Nor does it even necessarily involve infallibility, as I define that term. I affirm infallibility simply because the Bible seems to me describable in this way, not because it deductively follows from some doctrine of inspiration. But I confess that I am no more able to defend my theory of inspiration as an isolated doctrine (i.e., apart from looking at the phenomena of the Bible) than is the inerrantist. This is obviously because the Bible says nothing about the mode of inspiration or the logical implications of "Book x is inspired."

Nevertheless, I view inspiration in this way: "Inspiration" is that influence of the Holy Spirit on the Biblical writers *(a)* that what they wrote was a reliable and authoritative account of how God has revealed himself in history, and *(b)* that what they wrote was a reliable and authoritative theological interpretation of God's revelatory acts. This, in my opinion, makes the Bible unique among all the books that have ever been written, despite its human origin. God speaks to us in the Bible. Somehow, the Bible's words are God's words. This gives us a written record of God's revelation that is sufficient to make us "wise unto salvation" and to possess a theological standard that is profitable for teaching, reproof, correction, and training in righteousness.

The Old Testament prophets spoke as motivated by God, and their words were regarded as God's words (Ex. 4:30; 7:1–2; Deut. 31:19–22; II Sam. 23:2; I Kings 22:13–14; Jer. 1:9; 36:1–2; Ezek. 2:7; Hab. 2:2). Jesus attributed his words to the command of God (John 12:47–50). God is spoken of as the Bible's author (Heb. 3:7; 4:7), and Paul too claims that his words are from God (I Cor. 2:13; I Thess. 2:13). It is also interesting to note the phrases by which New Testament writers introduce quotations from the Old Testament. "The Holy Spirit says" (Heb. 3:7), "the Holy Spirit indicates" (Heb. 9:8), "God declares" (Acts 2:17), "what does the scripture say?" (Rom. 4:3; Gal. 4:30), and "it is written" (Matt. 4:7, 10) are typical. It seems clear that the New Testament writers regarded the Old Testament as divinely inspired (see also Gal. 3:8; Rom. 9:17). The human authors of the Old Testament are not forgotten, nor do the New

Testament writers forget human instrumentality in the writing of Scripture (Matt. 22:43; Acts 4:25).

2. The Bible also testifies to its own authority. If the words of the Scriptures are due to God (through the instrumentality of human beings), it is not surprising that these words are regarded as having divine authority and as being normative on all matters on which they touch. The Scriptures are recognized as standing forever. Isaiah says, "The grass withers, the flower fades; but the word of our God will stand for ever" (Isa. 40:8). The author of I Peter, quoting these words, adds: "That word is the good news which was preached to you" (I Peter 1:25). The psalmist says, "For ever, O LORD, thy word is firmly fixed in the heavens" (Ps. 119:89). Jesus says, "Scripture cannot be broken" (John 10:35), and "Till heaven and earth pass away, not an iota, not a dot, will pass from the law until all is accomplished" (Matt. 5:18).

Jesus viewed his words as possessing divine authority, the same authority which the Old Testament has. Mark records Jesus as saying, "Heaven and earth will pass away, but my words will not pass away" (Mark 13:31). Luke has him claim that the criterion by which a person was to be judged wise or unwise was whether or not that person heard and obeyed his words (Luke 6:47–49). And in a remarkable passage in John's Gospel, Jesus claims further that his words were given by God and thus that they possess divine authority:

> If any one hears my sayings and does not keep them, I do not judge him; for I did not come to judge the world but to save the world. He who rejects me and

does not receive my sayings has a judge; the word that
I have spoken will be his judge on the last day. For I
have not spoken on my own authority; the Father who
sent me has himself given me commandment what to
say and what to speak. (John 12:47–50; cf. also 3:34)

The apostles, and especially Paul, make similar
claims about their words. The Holy Spirit had been
promised them in a special way to guide them into
the truth (Matt. 10:19–20; Luke 12:12; John 14:26;
16:12–14), and they claim that their words are inspired by God and therefore binding. Thus we find
them making strong statements about the authority of
their words. Paul says that he is a "steward of the
mysteries of God" (I Cor. 4:1) and that his "gospel"
was given by a "revelation of Jesus Christ" (Gal.
1:11–12). For this reason, he insists on obedience to
his words:

But even if we, or an angel from heaven, should
preach to you a gospel contrary to that which we
preached to you, let him be accursed. As we have said
before, so now I say again, If any one is preaching to
you a gospel contrary to that which you received, let
him be accursed. (Gal. 1:8–9)

If any one thinks that he is a prophet, or spiritual, he
should acknowledge that what I am writing to you is
a command of the Lord. If any one does not recognize
this, he is not recognized. (I Cor. 14:37–38)

Paul refers to "the authority which the Lord has given
me for building up and not for tearing down" (II Cor.
13:10). Speaking of the instructions in righteous living which he has given the Thessalonians, he says,
"Whoever disregards this, disregards not man but

God, who gives his Holy Spirit to you" (I Thess. 4:8). And again to the Thessalonians he says, "If any one refuses to obey what we say in this letter, note that man, and have nothing to do with him, that he may be ashamed" (II Thess. 3:14; cf. 2:15 and I Cor. 11:2). The writer of I John apparently feels the same way about his words: "We are of God. Whoever knows God listens to us, and he who is not of God does not listen to us. By this we know the spirit of truth and the spirit of error" (I John 4:6). The New Testament writers, then, regard themselves as God's chosen messengers, entrusted with the message of reconciliation (II Cor. 5:19). As with the Old Testament prophets, they are God's chosen spokesmen: their words are ordained by God and are invested with his authority.

Another point should be noted: II Tim. 3:16 and II Peter 1:21, along with many other New Testament passages, show the high regard the New Testament writers have for the Old Testament. The "sacred writings" with which Timothy was acquainted from childhood can only be the Old Testament. They view it as inspired by God and as having divine authority. But they also regard their own words as being on an equal plane with the Old Testament. We can see this in II Peter, whose writer refers to the letters of Paul. He says that they are "hard to understand," and are "twisted" by the ignorant and unstable, *"as they do the other scriptures"* (II Peter 3:16, italics mine). Again, the "other scriptures" doubtless refer to the Old Testament, and thus the writer of II Peter seems literally to be canonizing the writings of Paul and placing them on a level with the Old Testament.

Paul also seems to view his own epistles in this way,

for he tells the Thessalonians: "I adjure you by the Lord that this letter be read to all the brethren" (I Thess. 5:27). And he says to the Colossians (Col. 4:16): "And when this letter has been read among you, have it read also in the church of the Laodiceans; and see that you read also the letter from Laodicea." What is the significance of this? Simply that *public* reading of a book was one of the early church's criteria for including a book in the canon of Scripture. Many writings were regarded as profitable for the Christian in *private* reading, but only books definitely considered inspired and divinely authoritative were publicly read in worship services. At the time of the writing of I Thessalonians and Colossians (still fairly early in the apostolic age) the only books that were universally read publicly at Christian gatherings were Old Testament books. They were read because they were regarded as Christian books, fully inspired by God. When Paul makes these statements, therefore, it seems that he regards his own writings as equal in inspiration and authority with the books of the Old Testament.

3. Finally, the Bible testifies to its own reliability or trustworthiness. We see this mainly in the attitude of the New Testament toward the Old Testament. Despite Jesus' willingness to disagree with the standard scribal interpretation of the Old Testament (see Matt. 5:21–48), despite Paul's view that the Christian is free from the Old Testament law (Gal. 3:1 to 5:12), and despite the claim of the writer of Hebrews that the law has been replaced in Christ by something better (Heb. 7:11–28), still there is never any tendency in the New Testament to deny, question, or criticize the Old Tes-

tament. That Old Testament prophecies have been fulfilled in Christ is claimed constantly (among many other passages, see Matt. 1:22; 2:15, 17, 23; 13:14, 35; John 12:38; Acts 1:16; 2:24–25). The historicity of events and figures described in the Old Testament is taken for granted: Adam and Eve (Matt. 19:4), Cain and Abel (Luke 11:51), the flood (Matt. 24:37–39), Sodom and Lot's wife (Luke 17:28–30, 32), manna in the Sinai (John 6:31–33), the brass serpent (John 3:14), and Jonah and the great fish (Matt. 12:39–41). Even the detailed wording of Old Testament texts is used to settle arguments. See Matt. 22:29–32, where the tense of an Old Testament verb is used by Jesus to prove a point against the Sadducees. See also John 10:34–36, where Jesus replies to the charge of blasphemy by citing the five words from Ps. 82:6: "I say, 'You are gods.' " The Old Testament is looked upon by New Testament writers as eternally relevant and as having been written for their benefit. Paul says, "For whatever was written in former days was written for our instruction, that by steadfastness and by the encouragement of the scriptures we might have hope" (Rom. 15:4). Referring to the events of the Israelite wanderings in the Sinai, he says, "Now these things happened to them as a warning, but they were written down for our instruction" (I Cor. 10:11; see also II Tim. 3:15–16, quoted earlier).

So the Bible clearly does hold a high view of itself. Does it teach inerrancy? Obviously not. There is offered in the Bible no definition of "inerrancy" or of any synonym, nor is there any statement of the doctrine. The only passages I can find in the Bible that come close are these:

Every word of God proves true. (Prov. 30:5)

This [the disciple whom Jesus loved] is the disciple who is bearing witness to these things, and who has written these things; and we know that his testimony is true. (John 21:24)

This I admit to you, that according to the Way, which they call a sect, I worship the God of our fathers, believing everything laid down by the law or written in the prophets. (Acts 24:14)

The first sentence is probably taken from Ps. 18:30 ("The promise of the LORD proves true") and is undoubtedly connected with the Biblical notion that God cannot lie (Num. 23:19; Titus 1:2). It says: God is our hope; in him we can trust with absolute confidence. I heartily concur with this. But the Bible containing an error is not the same thing as God lying. (The question, "But can God lie?" is sometimes used as a rhetorical device by unsophisticated defenders of inerrancy.)

The second sentence occurs at the conclusion of the Fourth Gospel. I do not wish to enter here the debate over who wrote this Gospel; suffice it to say that these words are designed to authenticate and vouch for the eyewitness accuracy of the book (cf. John 19:35). But they do not teach that the Bible or even the Fourth Gospel is inerrant.

The third sentence is from Paul's speech before Felix. I have no doubt that Paul believed just as he said he believed. What he is establishing here—as he does elsewhere (Rom. 11:1; Phil. 3:5–6)—are his Jewish credentials. He is saying that he has not deviated from the faith of Israel and that as far as the trustworthiness of the Old Testament is concerned, he now believes just as he has always believed.

So it is clear that the Bible does not teach that it is inerrant, despite the claims of some that it does. There is no definition of the term, no statement of the doctrine, no use of such philosophical arguments as the epistemological argument or the slippery slide argument, and the problem passages that have led some to deny that the Bible is inerrant are not dealt with. The Bible does not teach inerrancy, nor does inerrancy seem to be presupposed or implied by what it does teach. There are those, however, who think otherwise. Let us now look at their argument.

DOES INSPIRATION DEMAND INERRANCY?

Recognizing perhaps that the Bible does not explicitly teach inerrancy, some inerrantists retire to the second and more complex form of the Biblical argument. It is often stated this way: "A book is inspired if and only if it is inerrant; the Bible teaches that it is inspired; so the Bible is inerrant." In his article "The Infallible Word," for example, Lindsell says: "Once it has been established that the Scriptures are 'breathed out by God,' it follows axiomatically that the books of the Bible are free from error and trustworthy in every regard."[36] He expresses this argument more thoroughly in *The Battle for the Bible*. Reduced to its essential propositions, the argument comes out something like this:

4. God inspired the Scriptures (II Tim. 3:16).

5. "Inspired" = "God so worked in the minds

and hearts of the writers that he got written
what he wanted."

6. God cannot lie.

7. Therefore, Scriptures are inerrant, i.e., do not
   lie.

   Or, more simply:

8. God's word cannot lie.

9. The Bible is God's word.

10. Therefore, the Bible cannot lie.

Are these sound arguments? Possibly they are
sound when based on *some* theories of inspiration.
They might stand on a mechanical dictation theory,
wherein the Biblical writers passively copied down
exactly what God whispered in their ears. But I know
of no inerrantist today who admits to holding such a
view of inspiration. For this theory is inconsistent with
what we know today about the origin of the books of
the Bible. Many were compiled from sources—older
documents, public registers, genealogies, histories of
kings, literary or liturgical sources, oral tradition—
which themselves were incomplete, erroneous, or inconsistent with one another. And the fallibility of
these sources is in places reflected in the Bible (e.g.,
in the statistical and other discrepancies between II
Sam. 24:1, 9, and I Chron. 21:1, 5, or between II Sam.
24:24 and I Chron. 21:25). Of course an inerrantist
can claim that these are not real discrepancies—i.e.,
that the Holy Spirit through inspiration miraculously
corrected whatever flaws existed in the sources relied

on by the Biblical writers. But the Bible clearly claims no such thing in its doctrine of inspiration, and the discrepancies look to be quite real.

This second version of the Biblical argument is deductive in the extreme. Rather than an open-minded *looking to see* what kind of Bible God inspired and building a doctrine of inspiration from it, this argument posits *a priori* the principle that if the Bible is inspired it must be inerrant. Surely it is unwise to try to tell God what kind of Bible he must have produced if he really wanted an inspired Bible. The wiser course is simply to look and see what sort of Bible he *has* produced. I would claim that an open-minded look at the Bible *does* support the claim that it is inspired (I agree with Warfield that the indicia are impressive) and *does not* support the claim that it is inerrant. If this is so, it follows that the second form of the Biblical argument fails.

Moreover, we know from the history of the doctrine of inspiration how dangerous deduction can be. Fuller points out several claims about the Bible, once deductively promulgated, that have now had to be given up:

> Quenstedt declared that Luke did not write from memory or from what others related to him, but by dictation of the Holy Spirit, who suggested to his mind the thoughts and words which he should use. In 1659 the theological faculty of Wittenberg condemned Beza's view that New Testament Greek contained barbarisms and solecisms. Gerhard argued that the Hebrew vowel points were inspired. John Owen thought that the Holy Spirit had kept the Hebrew and Greek texts pure throughout all textual transmission.[37]

The Bible surely was produced through the instrumentality of its human authors, who themselves were
fallible. They wrote with their theological convictions,
cultural and historical frames of reference, and stylistic
idiosyncracies intact. I do not deny *a priori* that the
Holy Spirit *could have* produced an inerrant Bible by
use of inspiration (despite the instrumentality of fallible human authors) had he chosen to do so. What I
deny is the reasonableness of the claim that this is in
fact what he *did* do. The Bible does not claim that he
did so, nor do the phenomena support this claim.
Thus, again, we see that the second form of the Biblical argument must be mistaken.

Finally, it seems to me that the inerrantists' limita-
tion of inerrancy to the autographs throws the Biblical
argument out of joint. If a book is inspired if and only
if it is inerrant, as they claim, then why is it that Jesus,
Paul, and others are prepared to claim that the Old
Testament Scriptures are inspired? It is almost certain
that they never saw an Old Testament autograph, and
they make no use of the notion of autographs in their
comments about the Scriptures. The inference seems
compelling that the New Testament writers regarded
fallible copies and even fallible translations such as the
Septuagint (a third century B.C. translation of the Old
Testament into Greek) as inspired. Paul even calls the
Septuagint "scripture" (the same word that is used in
II Tim. 3:16, where it is said that Scripture is "God-
breathed"), for in Rom. 4:3 he prefaces a slightly
altered quotation of the Septuagint of Gen. 15:6 with
the question, "What does the scripture say?"[38] Paul
apparently regarded the Septuagint as Scripture, and
he regarded all Scripture as inspired. Thus if a writing

is inspired if and only if it is inerrant—as inerrantists claim—it must follow that the Septuagint is inerrant. This looks like a good deduction, except that it is universally recognized that the Septuagint is *not* inerrant. In places it is quite inaccurate. Thus the inerrantists' deduction fails.

We can conclude, then, that the Bible teaches that it is inspired, authoritative, and trustworthy. But it neither teaches, implies, nor presupposes that it is inerrant.

3

THE
EPISTEMOLOGICAL
ARGUMENT

THE SECOND MAJOR ARGUMENT for inerrancy is what I call "the epistemological argument." This argument, appealed to by many defenders of inerrancy, appears in several different forms. The basic idea is quite clear: Unless the Bible is inerrant, Christians have no sound epistemological foundation on which to base their beliefs. Thus inerrancy is crucial for Christians.

The various forms of the epistemological argument are seldom carefully distinguished, and are usually conflated by those who use the argument. All forms of the argument are related to the central idea stated above. Nevertheless, a few distinct versions of it can be detected. I will call them EA1, EA2, EA3, and EA4.

> EA1 If the Bible is errant, we have no sure word from God, for if the Bible errs in some passages, it might err in any passage, and so can nowhere be relied upon.[39]

> EA2 The Bible is supposed to be authoritative for Christians in all matters of faith and practice, and if the Bible is inerrant, it is obvious

how it can be authoritative in this way. But if the Bible is errant, it cannot be authoritative for Christian faith and practice in the required way.[40]

EA3 If the Bible is errant, we have no sure source or standard in theology. Each person must find his own extra-Biblical criterion for faith and practice, i.e., his criterion for deciding what in the Bible is to be believed and what is not to be believed. This criterion, whatever it is, will in effect be superior to the Bible. And the notion that there is a criterion of faith and practice superior to the Bible is unchristian.[41]

EA4 Inerrancy is the only sure guarantee that other Christian beliefs are true. If the Bible is errant, we have no such sure guarantee.[42]

I do not find any of these arguments compelling. There is truth in some of them, but as arguments for inerrancy, I do not believe they will stand. I will now try to show why. In replying to the epistemological argument, I have decided not to try to handle each form of the argument separately. The arguments flow into and out of one another too easily for that. I do not believe I can answer any one of them without answering them all. So what I propose to do is make a general response to the epistemological argument, and hope that when I have finished I will have said something in reply to each of its forms as well.

How Firm a Foundation?

Let me begin by listing some propositions:

A. The Bible is inerrant.

B. We are lost in sin and need divine redemption.

C. Christ bodily rose from the dead on the third day.

D. Persons need to commit their lives in faith to Christ.

Can a Christian believe B, C, and D without believing A? Obviously, the answer to this is yes. And the reason I am quite sure that the answer is yes is that *I* believe B, C, and D and do not believe A. But perhaps this is not quite the point that the epistemological arguer wants to make. Perhaps he is asking this: Can we *know* B, C, and D without knowing A? The answer to this will depend on what is meant by the word "know." There are different meanings of the word. Descartes spoke of "knowing" a proposition if and only if that proposition is immune to any conceivable doubt. In this sense I seriously question whether anyone knows B, C, and D. I cannot claim to know them in this sense, though I certainly do believe them.

But if the word "know" means something weaker than this—e.g., if I know a proposition if and only if the proposition is true and I believe it on the basis of good reasons—I do not see why a person cannot know B, C, and D without knowing A. As a way of illustrating, let us consider the following propositions:

E. All that Smith says is true.

F. Smith says that Smith was born in What Cheer.

G. Smith says that Smith is a philosopher.

H. Smith says that Smith will quit smoking.

How are these propositions related to one another epistemologically? Well, several facts seem clear. For one thing, knowing E appears to be a way of learning certain facts about Smith. A person who knows E will believe that Smith was born in What Cheer, is a philosopher, and will quit smoking as soon as he hears Smith make these statements. So there does appear to be an epistemological relationship between E and F, G, and H that other propositions (say, "Elliott quotes Latin") do not bear to F, G, and H. Another fact also emerges: We do not have to argue about the truth value of "Smith was born in What Cheer," "Smith is a philosopher," and "Smith will quit smoking" if we know that E is true and that Smith made these statements. All of this seems clear but is quite irrelevant to the issue at hand. It is still obvious that a person can know F, G, H, and all that these propositions claim about Smith, without knowing E at all. It seems entirely possible for there to be a person who knows all of this but who has not the vaguest idea whether or not E is true.

Similarly, if A is true, and if it can be shown that the Bible does indeed teach B, C, and D, then we do not need to argue about the truth value of B, C, and D: we know that they are true. This much must be granted. But unfortunately this does not constitute much of an argument for believing A. It is still quite possible to believe and know (in the weaker sense) B, C, and D without knowing or even believing A at all.

Is it true, as EA4 claims, that inerrancy is the only "sure guarantee" that doctrines like B, C, and D are true? Again, this will depend on what is meant by the term "sure guarantee." And again, there is a curious parallel with Descartes here. As is well known, in the *Meditations*[43] Descartes seems to accept this principle: If there is a source of knowledge that has ever misled me in the past (i.e., given me false information), it is no longer trustworthy, because it might at any point mislead me again. Thus those who use the epistemological argument are saying, I believe, that if the Bible is shown to be errant, it might be false at any point. The answer to this is that the Bible *might* mislead us at any point whether we believe in inerrancy or not. The only way we can know that it will never mislead us is if we know that it is inerrant, which in my opinion no one knows. I do not believe we have any "sure guarantee" that *any* Christian doctrine is true—at least not a Cartesian sort of "sure guarantee." We do have evidence, and I am a Christian because I believe that the available evidence, both subjective and objective, supports Christian beliefs. But more than this we do not have.

Carl Henry speaks of the "epistemological credentials" of Christian beliefs. He says, "The real question is whether, once scriptural errancy is affirmed, a consistent evangelical faith is maintained thereafter only by an act of will rather than by persuasive epistemological credentials."[44] In other words, he holds that evangelicals like me who believe doctrines like B, C, and D without believing A do so only as an act of will: Their epistemological presuppositions, I take him to be saying, should really lead them to deny B, C, and

D. But I believe that the only epistemological credentials a doctrine must have in order to be accepted by evangelicals is that it seem true on the available evidence. It is not a matter of one who does not believe in inerrancy accepting evangelical doctrines as a sheer act of will—in fact, I'm not even sure what "believing something by an act of will" amounts to. Nor do I see how his rejection of inerrancy should lead the evangelical to reject his other doctrines. He accepts them simply because they seem true to him (just as the believer in inerrancy accepts *his* beliefs because they seem true to him). And, pre-eminently, they "seem true to him" if they are taught in the Bible. I believe B, C, and D because I believe they are taught in the Bible and because I know of no argument or evidence that refutes them. In my opinion, this is all the epistemological credentials a doctrine needs or can have.

At this point EA2 and EA3 will be brought in by the defender of inerrancy: "If you do not believe that the Bible is inerrant," he will say, "it is not enough merely to show that B, C, and D are taught in the Bible, for the places where these doctrines are taught in the Bible may be the very places the Bible errs. So how do you decide what in the Bible you are going to accept and what you are going to reject? How can an errant Bible be authoritative?"

I confess there is an element of truth in these arguments. It is true that no Christian who believes that the Bible errs can hold that the Bible *alone* is his authority for faith and practice. He must hold to some other authority or criterion as well. That authority, I am not embarrassed to say, is his own mind, his own ability to reason. But I also believe that the defender of inerrancy is only fooling himself when he says, by contrast, that the Bible is indeed *his* only authority. As I will show, reason is equally a criterion for him too. There is *no one,* in my opinion, for whom the Bible *alone* is his authority of Christian faith and practice.

I should add two notes here. First, I do affirm the traditional Christian claim that the Holy Spirit guides us into truth, although I do not wish to explore here the question of how this guidance works in relation to Scripture, reason, or any other epistemological authority. And second, I am aware of, and agree with, the notion of Luther and Calvin that sin has corrupted all aspects of human personality, including reason, and that reason is not therefore an infallible guide to truth. It is fallible and can be used for evil ends. But does this mean that I should "mistrust my reason" in the sense of embracing apparently irrational propositions or rejecting apparently rational ones? Of course not. Corrupted or not, we have no choice but to listen to and follow the dictates of reason. This is true of all of us, not just those who deny that anyone can base faith and practice on the Bible alone. So far as I can tell, not even the most vehement advocates of *sola scriptura*—the doctrine that the Bible should be the only authority on religious matters—are inclined to believe irrational things, e.g., that $2 + 2 = 7$ or that Seaman Hall levitates twice nightly. And I take it that this means that reason is for them too a criterion of what should and should not be believed.

No doubt this point will still be disputed by some, but it can be seen quite easily. Let us recall for a moment Lindsell's struggle with the different accounts of Peter's denial. What precisely does the Bible teach on the disputed point, i.e., on the number of times the cock crowed? The answer seems clear: The Bible teaches both that the cock crowed once (Matthew, Luke, John) *and* that the cock crowed twice (Mark). Thus anyone who claims that the Bible *alone* is his authority must believe nothing else than that the cock crowed once and that it crowed twice, which of course is a contradiction. To his credit, Lindsell cannot believe this, and so he attempts to reconcile the accounts, as we saw. He cannot believe this, I submit, because like all rational persons he finds himself unable to believe contradictions. So we can see that he too has another criterion besides the Bible for what he will or will not believe. That criterion is his own mind. I believe this is true of all Christians, not just of Lindsell and myself.

The inerrantist will protest that there is a distinction that must be made. He is using his mind to help him *determine what the Bible says,* not *whether or not he will believe* what the Bible says. That is, he will protest that the debate has shifted from the reliability of the Bible to hermeneutics. I must admit that this is quite true. But it does nothing to mitigate my simple point that even for the believer in inerrancy reason is a criterion for what he will or will not believe.

This can be seen in another way as well. Francis Schaeffer is a firm defender of inerrancy. In his book *No Final Conflict* he advises Christians on what to do where there are apparent conflicts between Biblical claims and current scientific theories:

> There is a tendency among many today to consider that the scientific truth will always be more true. This

we must reject. We must take ample time, and sometimes this will mean a long time, to consider whether
the apparent clash between science and revelation
means that the theory set forth by science is wrong or
whether we must reconsider what we thought the
Bible says.[45]

I am not sure what it is for one truth to be "more true"
than another. Nevertheless I can endorse part of Schaeffer's meaning: Some Christians are altogether too
ready to jettison Biblical claims whenever they seem
to conflict with the latest beliefs of scientists. But what
Schaeffer's words clearly show is that even for the
person who accepts inerrancy, reason is a criterion
helping him determine what he will or will not believe. For in places of conflict between science and
Scripture, he must either reject the scientific theory or
else reinterpret Scripture. Where they are inconsistent
he cannot believe both. He must use his mind to determine how Scripture can be interpreted in such a way
that he can still believe it.

The question might then be asked, How do I view
the Bible as authoritative for Christian faith and practice? My belief is that the Bible is infallible on matters
of faith and practice and that it is amazingly reliable,
but not inerrant, on all other matters. As I noted in the
Preface, my willingness to affirm the infallibility of the
Bible does not mean I understand everything the
Bible says on matters of faith and practice. There are
some items which I confess I do not understand.
Nevertheless, I have an extremely strong sense that I
have never been misled by the Bible on matters of
faith and practice, and a sense of having been gripped
and greatly influenced by its message and by the Lord

it reveals. I believe it is a Christian's responsibility to accept *whatever* the Bible says on *any subject whatsoever* unless there is compelling reason not to accept it. That is, everything in the Bible is authoritative and normative for the Christian until he comes across a passage which for good reasons he cannot accept.

Lindsell quotes with approval these words from Augustine:

> Freely do I admit . . . that I have learnt to ascribe to those Books which are of canonical rank, and only to them, such reverence and honour, that I firmly believe that no single error due to the author is found in any one of them. And when I am confronted in these books with anything that seems to be at variance with truth, I do not hesitate to put it down either to the use of an incorrect text, or to the failure of a commentator rightly to explain the words, or to my own mistaken understanding of the passage.[46]

I cannot agree with everything that Augustine says here, but I do agree that where one has difficulty accepting what the Bible says in a given text, one ought not easily jump to the conclusion that the Bible is wrong. One's first impulse probably ought to be: "The Bible is correct and I am wrong." One should reject something that the Bible says only where, having thoroughly examined the problem, in all humility one cannot accept what it says. It is not a matter of accepting what I like or agree with or happen to find illuminating and rejecting the rest. Of course, I am the final judge of what I will believe or not believe (though this is true of the inerrantist too), and I must take responsibility for what I decide to believe or not believe. But it is not just a matter of taste, like deciding between different flavors of ice cream ("What speaks to me is God's word and what does not is not"). The work of theology and exegesis obviously enter in. In a sense, the whole community of Christian believers helps me to decide what I will believe, whether or not there is compelling reason to reject some Biblical claim. For me this does not occur often, but it does occur occasionally. It has never yet occurred on a matter of faith or practice, and, like Fuller, I hope it never will.

"But if the Bible is mistaken in one place, it may be mistaken at any place," the EA1 arguer will say. It is true that the Bible *may* be mistaken at any point. But that does not mean it *is,* nor do I see how it follows from this that it is no longer trustworthy. For example, I happen to have a great deal of trust in the reliability and truthfulness of my wife, but that does not mean she is inerrant. Like any human being, she makes mistakes, and like me and probably every other person, she has probably made untrue statements. If this means she *might* be unreliable in anything that she says, I will have to agree, but I cannot see how this is supposed to mitigate my trust in her. Though my reliance on her word is not as great as my reliance on God's word—she does not claim to be inspired—it is true of her too that despite her fallibility, I will believe whatever she says unless and until I have convincing reason not to believe her.

"But if your policy is to accept whatever the Bible says unless there is convincing evidence not to do so, you can never know that what you *accept* from the Bible is true: it might be open to convincing but presently unknown objections." This also is true but irrelevant. The sort of absolutely certain Cartesian knowledge that is being spoken of here—belief that is immune to any imaginable doubt—is nowhere to be had outside of logic and mathematics, and so it does not amount to much of a criticism to assert that my theology prevents me from attaining it. Not even the inerrantist knows in this way that what he believes is true. For in his own way he is open to an analogous objection: "You do not know that what you accept from a given Biblical text is true, because your interpretation of the text might be open to convincing but presently unknown objections."

No Bible Is Inerrant

I think it can thus be seen that the epistemological argument is at best inconclusive and at worst virtually useless as an argument for inerrancy. I am aware that what I have said in this chapter will convince few advocates of inerrancy. I know from experience that it is difficult for believers and nonbelievers in the doctrine to communicate with one another on this point. The one just can't see how an errant Bible can provide a proper epistemological base for Christian theology and the other is unable to understand quite what the problem is supposed to be or what a "proper epistemological base" is. At one point in my career I spent a year at Fuller Theological Seminary, where I was fortunate enough to come to know the late Professor Edward John Carnell. Carnell was an advocate of Biblical inerrancy and was quite articulate in saying why. He was, however, disinclined to expel non-inerrantist evangelicals from any camp. We had several discussions on inerrancy, but they always seemed to reach an impasse at the point of the authority of an errant Bible. I always had the feeling we understood each other's positions quite well up to that point, but at that point we always seemed to lose each other.

Thus far I have been defending my own position against the various forms of the epistemological argument. Let me now move from the defensive to the offensive and present an argument of roughly the same sort *against* inerrancy.

To my knowledge, no contemporary defender of inerrancy claims that presently existing Bibles are inerrant; what is claimed is that the autographs were inerrant. They were inerrant, so it is said, because God inspired the writers so that what they wrote was without error. But everybody admits that presently existing Bibles contain errors, and the obvious conclusion to be drawn from this is that since God did not miraculously keep the copyists from making transmissional errors, God must not think it vital that Christians have an inerrant text.

Furthermore, it does not seem clear why we need an inerrant Bible. As we have seen, even those who admit that present Bibles contain errors and who retire to a doctrine of inerrant autographs have to admit that the church has existed for nearly two thousand years on the basis of non-autographs, i.e., errant Biblical texts. I was raised in the church and came to a position of faith on the basis of an errant Bible, and so did every other Christian living today. The work of the church has gone on these twenty centuries and will continue. Why do we need more than this?

The inerrantist might object to this as follows: "Transmissional errors are in principle correctable by textual criticism but errors in autographs are not. So God leaves it up to us to produce a text that is an accurate reproduction of the autographs, but he obviously cannot leave it up to us to produce an inerrant autograph. *He* had to do that, which he did by inspiring the original writers of the Bible." I can agree with the first sentence of this objection—it seems a sound distinction. But the second is highly speculative and dubious. Even if the first sentence is true, what is supposed to follow from it? One must still wonder— if having an inerrant Bible is as crucial as defenders of inerrancy imply—why God didn't somehow ensure that we today possess an inerrant text, either the Biblical autographs themselves or else flawless copies of them. The obvious answer, since to the best of my knowledge no Christian since the time of Paul has ever even seen an autograph or a flawless copy, is that God does not agree with the defenders of inerrancy on the importance of our having an inerrant Bible.

Lindsell attempts to reply to this by arguing that God intended that the autographs not be preserved, lest believers be tempted idolatrously to revere or even worship them. He says that this very thing has occurred in Sikhism, whose sacred writing, the *Granth,* is displayed in such a way as to call attention to the book itself. But, obviously, Christians are to worship God, not the Bible.[47] I have no wish to argue that God *should* somehow have preserved the autographs or flawless copies of them. All I claim is that this seems to follow from the epistemological argument for inerrancy: If having an inerrant Bible is as crucial as the inerrantist implies, one must wonder why God didn't ensure that we have an inerrant Bible. But Lindsell's response is feeble. For one thing, even if he is correct that our possessing Biblical autographs might lead to our illicit worship of them, God could easily have solved this problem by allowing the autographs to disappear (which is in fact what he did do) and ensuring the preservation of flawless copies of them. And for another, I doubt that even Lindsell's main point is worth worrying about. Let us suppose for a moment that all the Biblical autographs have been miraculously preserved by God and that they are now on display in the Institute of Antiquity and Christianity in Claremont. Would Christians be tempted to worship these manuscripts? Not if they took seriously what the manuscripts themselves would say, for the Bible condemns idolatry as sin. So properly honoring whatever autographs God preserved would entail *not* worshiping them. This is a rather obvious point, and I think most Christians would recognize it.

One final matter: Inerrantists claim that if a book is inspired it is inerrant. But to my knowledge, no contemporary defender of inerrancy claims that the Bible was written in grammatically perfect Hebrew or Greek. Why not? Wouldn't it seem that inspiration (especially *verbal* inspiration, which all inerrantists espouse) would guarantee perfect grammar as well as perfect truthfulness? Not so, they would claim: "God didn't need perfect grammar to fulfill his intention of producing a book that truthfully communicates the ideas, facts, and injunctions that he wanted communicated to human beings; but he did need perfect truthfulness to do so."

But this is not true. God clearly does communicate his truth to people today, despite the fact that our access is limited to non-autographs, which inerrantists admit are errant. Thus it seems false to say that God must have an inerrant Bible if he is to communicate to us. "But if God did produce an inerrant Bible on matters of faith and practice, as you yourself claim, why didn't he do so on matters of history and science?" The answer to this is that there was, in my view, no need for God to produce an inerrant Bible on *any* subject. What I believe he did have to produce is a generally reliable and trustworthy Bible, reliable enough to convince people to believe what it says.

Some inerrantists seem to fear that when inerrancy collapses, Christianity collapses too. This fear is groundless. Christianity has not collapsed, though inerrancy is not now universally believed by Christians, if it ever was. Nor does there appear to be any good reason to hold that inerrancy is a necessary presupposition to the great doctrines of the Bible. What Christians want, obviously, is for non-Christians to believe these doctrines. Belief in inerrancy does not appear necessary either to believe or to defend these doctrines. Even Carnell, staunch defender of inerrancy that he was, seemed to see this:

> It is extremely difficult, if not impossible, to coax all the Biblical data into neat harmony. But this want of precision in no way affects the substance of the Biblical system.[48]

If the phenomenological difficulties that we find in the Bible and our inability to defend inerrancy in no way destroy the acceptability of "the Biblical system," then it appears that inerrancy is not a necessary requisite for accepting this system. If this is a proper inference from what Carnell is saying, I agree with him. The great doctrines of the Bible on which Christianity is based do not require or presuppose inerrancy.

I should note here that the epistemological argument is no more a good defense of my notion of infallibility than it is of inerrancy. If some Biblical teaching on Christian faith and practice is shown to be mistaken, then not only is that particular teaching in error but I am in error in affirming that the Bible, in my sense, is infallible. But not even this necessarily means that the whole edifice of Christianity comes tumbling down. That will happen only if some Biblical teaching on which the whole edifice of Christianity depends is falsified, for example, the resurrection of Jesus Christ from the dead. So my position is not that God *had* to produce an infallible Bible. I just claim that as far as I can tell, that is what in fact he *did* do.

4

THE
SLIPPERY SLIDE
ARGUMENT

EVANGELICAL CHRISTIANS are seriously concerned about theology, and rightly so. This interest in maintaining doctrinal integrity occasionally is expressed in what I call the slippery slide argument (SSA for short). Its essential form is something like this:

> Belief in doctrine A is crucial for Christians because those who reject it are likely also to doubt doctrines B, C, and D, which places them on the slippery slide that leads to liberalism and ultimately to no faith at all.

Theoretically, A, B, C, and D could be any doctrines of Christianity, but the SSA is perhaps most often presented as an argument in support of the claim that the Bible is inerrant. For our present purposes, then, let us say that the letters A, B, C, and D stand for the same propositions that they represented in Chapter 3:

A. The Bible is inerrant.

B. We are lost in sin and need divine redemption.

C. Christ bodily rose from the dead on the third day.

   D. Persons need to commit their lives in faith to
       Christ.

It should be noted that B, C, and D could stand for any
doctrines typically held by evangelicals and considered crucial by them.

Understanding the Argument

   Is the SSA a sound argument? Well, one immediate
problem is that it is not clear precisely what it is supposed to mean. So I propose now four possible meanings it might be said to have. Then I will examine each
to see if the SSA, however it is interpreted, is a strong
argument.

   1. The SSA might mean something like this: "The
person who does not believe A is *logically forced* to deny
B, C, and D—i.e., any rational person who denies A
must also deny B, C, and D." But this claim does not
seem to be true at all. At least I can see no logical
reasons pushing the rational person who denies A toward denying B, C, and D. These doctrines clearly do
not logically entail A. This claim *would* be true if instead of A, B, C, and D we had:

   E. Bill Jones is mortal.

   F. All men named Bill are mortal.

   G. All men named Jones are mortal.

   H. All men are mortal.

Assuming that there are men and that Bill Jones is a
man, it appears true that any rational person who de-

nies E also denies F, G, and H. This is because E is entailed by each of the other propositions (together with the stipulated assumptions).

But obviously the relationship between A, B, C, and D is not like this. It is quite true that evangelical Christians believe B, C, and D (and many other doctrines as well) because they are taught in the Bible. The Bible is, after all, supposed to be the source of and authority for all Christian beliefs. But I see no reason to say that the person who denies A is logically or morally no longer allowed to use the Bible as the source of and authority for his beliefs. Thus, on this interpretation of the SSA, the argument is unconvincing.

2. Perhaps, then, it means something like this: "The person who rejects A *will be caused* by this rejection also to reject B, C, and D (and other doctrines crucial to evangelical Christianity); i.e., the person who does not believe A will at some later point in his life also give up belief in B, C, and D (and other doctrines crucial to evangelical Christianity)." This interpretation seems to capture well the "slide" metaphor of the SSA. It suggests a notion of inability to stop oneself from slipping down the theological slide. But even so, this interpretation is not true. We know that it is not true because there have been many Christians who have lived and died who affirmed B, C, and D and did not affirm A. There are also a good many living evangelicals who, like me, do not affirm A and who have no intention of giving up their belief in such doctrines as B, C, and D. In general, it is difficult to see how a person's failing to hold a given belief can *cause* him to

give up other beliefs that he holds. Now perhaps the slippery slide arguer can somehow make sense of this notion. But if he is actually predicting that anyone who accepts B, C, and D and who does not accept A will at some future point in his life reject B, C, and D, then he is clearly mistaken.

3. Perhaps the SSA means something like this: "The person who denies A is *open to the possibility* of denying B, C, and D in a way in which the person who affirms A is not." I can readily grant that this sentence may be true. Even so, it does not constitute much of an argument for the truth of A, for the person who *affirms* A can also be open to the possibility of denying B, C, and D, though perhaps in a slightly different way. To be fair with the slippery slide arguer we should admit that it might be psychologically easier for at least some people to deny B, C, and D if they also deny A— easier, that is, than if they affirm A. But, again, it is possible for a person both to affirm A and to deny B, C, and D by interpreting his inerrant Bible differently from the way evangelical Christians typically do. Mormons, for example, believe that the Bible is inerrant, but are certainly not evangelical Christians.

Nevertheless it must be admitted that the following propositions seem true:

> I. Most people who believe A also believe B, C, and D,
>
>   and
>
> J. Most people who deny B, C, and D also deny A.

If, as I admit, I and J are true, they constitute psychologically interesting facts about the beliefs of certain people, but are they anything more than this? I do not see that they are. I and J would probably also be true if B, C, and D remain as they are and if for A we read not "The Bible is inerrant" but "The creation occurred in 4004 B.C." Fortunately these days one does not often hear people arguing on behalf of this proposition, either by means of the SSA or any other argument. Thus, since I and J fail to constitute good reasons for affirming that the creation occurred in 4004 B.C., these propositions also fail to constitute good reasons for affirming that the Bible is inerrant.

4. Finally, perhaps the SSA ought to be taken as an argument about evangelical Christian *groups* rather than individuals. It may mean something like this: "Any evangelical Christian group that gives up A as part of its creed or criteria for membership will have some members who will give up doctrines like B, C, and D. If A is affirmed by the group, the continued holding of doctrines like B, C, and D by its members is at least *possible;* but if A is not affirmed by the group, the future abandonment of doctrines like B, C, and D by at least some of its members is *virtually guaranteed.*"[49]

I find this a puzzling argument. One thing to notice about it is that it seems to make a much weaker claim than the earlier versions of the SSA. Another is that it doubtless contains an element of truth: no evangelical Christian group that omits A from its creed or membership criteria can guarantee that no future member will give up doctrines like B, C, and D. But then again, in my opinion, neither can any group which retains A. I strongly doubt that there exists *any* evangelical Christian group, whether it affirms A or not, that can boast that no member ever gave up doctrines like B, C, and D. But is it *possible* that a group that affirms A will perennially ensure the orthodoxy of its members? Yes, this is possible, though in my opinion highly improbable. It is also possible, though equally improbable, that a group that does *not* affirm A will do this too.

There simply is no way for any Christian or Christian group to guarantee today what Christians will or will not believe tomorrow. Of course evangelical creeds are needed, but they should not be seen as devices to ensure future orthodoxy. What evangelicals must do, in my opinion, is simply remake the case for evangelical theology each new generation, i.e., remake the case for believing doctrines like B, C, and D. I believe this is exactly what evangelical Christians have been doing since the first century. It is just not true that we can ensure or even increase the probability of future fidelity to evangelical beliefs by insisting on inerrancy today.

EXPLORING THE ARGUMENT FURTHER

This is the best attempt I can make to understand the thinking that lies behind the SSA. It does not seem an impressive argument however one tries to interpret it. Perhaps there is another way we can approach the matter. Let us now ask this question: What exactly is supposed to be wrong in the position of the person who affirms B, C, and D and denies A? Three possible answers come to mind. Let us examine each in turn.

One possible answer is that a person is just plain wrong in failing to affirm A, simply because A is *true*. A may be true, and let us suppose for a moment that it is. If A is true, then the position of the person who denies A is indeed a mistaken position in that he *should* affirm A, just as he should affirm every true doctrine. But even if A is true, and I do not believe it is, this does not support the SSA or show that the person who denies A and affirms B, C, and D is being inconsistent.

This suggests another possible answer to our question: Perhaps what is wrong in the position of the person who denies A and affirms B, C, and D is that in believing as he does he is being *inconsistent*. But I see no inconsistency here. A neither entails nor is entailed by B, C, and D. If we were talking about the following propositions, there would be an inconsistency:

H. All men are mortal.

K. Smith is mortal.

L. Brown is mortal.

M. Adams is mortal.

Assuming that Smith, Brown, and Adams are men, it is inconsistent to affirm H and deny K, L, and M simply because H (together with this assumption) logically entails K, L, and M. But Biblical inerrancy bears no such logical relationship to such doctrines as B, C, and D.

There is yet one final possible answer to this question: Perhaps what is wrong in the position of the person who denies A and affirms B, C, and D is that in denying A he is denying a doctrine that is *crucial to Christianity.* This answer is obviously dependent in part upon the first answer, at least for the Christian, who believes that Christianity is true. It is hard to see how a doctrine could be crucial for a true religion unless the doctrine itself were true. So what I said in response to that answer can be said here as well. But even more importantly, if the SSA actually implies that the evangelical Christian who denies A is on the road that leads to liberal Christianity and ultimately to non-Christianity, then it is clear that the SSA is based on a horrible mistake, viz., it confuses what one "does" with what one "might do." It may be true, in some sense, that the person who denies A *might* also deny B, C, and D, but so might a person who affirms A. But this does not mean that he necessarily *does* or *will* deny B, C, or D. Surely we are evangelical Christians not because of what we *might* believe or do, given our presuppositions, but because of what we *do* believe and do. Similarly, we come to know God not because we might commit our lives in faith to Christ but because we do.

Is It Taught in the Bible?

It seems to me that the SSA is simply based on a mistaken notion of how evangelicals are to decide what they are to believe. The real question to ask is whether or not a doctrine is true, not what the pragmatic effects of believing or not believing it will be. The pre-eminent way for the evangelical to answer this question in relation to any suggested doctrine is to ask whether or not the doctrine is either explicitly taught in the Bible or else is presupposed or implied by what is explicitly taught in the Bible. It must be noted, then, that the SSA does not appear in the Bible.[50]

Fortunately, we are not saved by the correctness of our theology, though obviously the correctness of our theology is relevant to our salvation. So even if the Bible *is* inerrant, it is hard to see why God would condemn those evangelicals who reject A. Furthermore, I do not believe that A is a claim that is made in the Bible. Doctrines B, C, and D, in my opinion, are taught in the Bible, but I can find nowhere in the Bible the claim that the Bible is free of all error. Thus, doctrines like B, C, and D are the sorts of doctrines to which we should turn in selecting criteria for what constitutes evangelical Christianity—not extra-Biblical, essentially apologetic notions like inerrancy.

I do sympathize with the plight of those evangelicals who wrestle with the question where to draw the dividing line between evangelical and nonevangelical Christianity. The instinct that leads them to notions like Biblical inerrancy is correct in at least some senses. It is quite true that the rise of Biblical criticism has been an important factor in the erosion of the strength of orthodoxy in the Christian church in the past century. It is also true, as I myself have observed, that those theologically immature evangelicals who take a religion course in college or a year in seminary and then jettison evangelical Christianity often do so on the basis of what they are told in the classroom about "the modern view of the Bible." And it is also true that people who deny doctrines like B, C, and D typically have a low view of the inspiration and authority of the Bible. But none of this, in my opinion, implies that inerrancy is a doctrine that must be held by evangelical Christians.

If the SSA has any validity at all, it is only in a much amended and weakened version. It is true that what leads evangelicals to accept doctrines like B, C, and D is their belief in the trustworthiness and authority of the Bible. So perhaps this version of the SSA is sound: For an evangelical who interprets the trustworthiness and authority of the Bible in terms of inerrancy, and who also believes that the Bible cannot be trustworthy or authoritative unless it is inerrant, doctrine A plays an epistemological role in his belief system that B, C, and D do not. If such a person gives up inerrancy and thus concludes that the Bible is neither trustworthy nor authoritative, he *might* give up B, C, and D as well.

But even if sound, this is obviously a frail reed on which to hang inerrancy. (1) It is not true that Biblical trustworthiness and authority depend upon inerrancy. (2) The amended version of the SSA applies to no one other than the person who once believed in the truth and importance of inerrancy. (3) The amended version does not even show that such a person *will* give up B, C, and D if he gives up A. What is to prevent him from retaining B, C, and D by adopting a different view of Biblical trustworthiness and authority from what he had before? (4) The amended version still says nothing about the truth of inerrancy but only about the pragmatic effects of believing it or not believing it.

What I conclude, then, is that the SSA is not a convincing argument in support of inerrancy. The SSA provides no reason for an evangelical to believe in inerrancy, let alone a reason to believe that inerrancy is essential to evangelical Christianity. I frankly doubt that the SSA is a convincing argument in favor of belief in any doctrine, and I therefore question its usefulness as an argumentative device in any context.

Furthermore, it is an insulting, divisive, and counterproductive argument. It is an affront to evangelicals like me who do not believe in inerrancy to be told that someday we will give up our evangelical beliefs. It suggests that the reason we do not believe in inerrancy is that our faith is weak or our commitment tenuous. It is divisive, because it implies that those who do not believe in inerrancy are not really evangelicals, thus encouraging believers in inerrancy to separate from and condemn such people. It is counterproductive, because it does more harm than good. Perhaps there are people who have been frightened by the SSA into repressing whatever doubts they may have about inerrancy. Whether or not this is a good thing I will not discuss here. But I am quite sure that there are at least an equal number, like the young man I mentioned in the Preface, who, despite doubts about inerrancy, might well have retained their evangelical identity, except that the SSA convinced them they were no longer evangelical.

I believe the abandonment of the SSA by all evangelicals would be a good thing. I hope the people who use this argument will stop.

5

THE CASE
AGAINST INERRANCY

REFUTING THE ARGUMENTS that are presented in favor of a given claim is not the same as refuting the claim itself. The claim may still be true, despite the weakness of the arguments given in its behalf. So now I must say why I cannot affirm that the Bible is inerrant. Accordingly, I will raise four arguments against inerrancy. They are:

1. The phenomena of Scripture do not support the claim that the Bible is inerrant.

2. The device of appealing to the intention of the Biblical writer (which is used by virtually every contemporary defender of inerrancy) raises more problems than it solves.

3. Inerrancy emphasizes the wrong tasks, e.g., defending obscure minutia in Scripture rather than proclaiming its message.

4. Inerrancy appears to make all of Christianity hang upon the successful completion of this "defending" enterprise.

I will now take up each argument and explain what I mean.

PHENOMENOLOGICAL DIFFICULTIES

1. The phenomena of Scripture do not support the claim that the Bible is inerrant. Let me say first that I do not relish the prospect of writing this section. I considered at one time omitting any section on the phenomena altogether, but I have decided that this would not be a responsible omission. To be honest with my readers I should indicate somewhere some of the Biblical passages I think are in error. There are two reasons for my apprehension. First, what I say here may give the impression to some that I approach Scripture with an unbelieving, superior attitude. That is not true. Second, I fear that some defenders of inerrancy will take my "Biblical errors" and superficially say something like: "Is *that* the worst you can do? I can solve these problems and can think of worse ones. If that's the basis for your case, the Bible must be inerrant after all."

There are, in fact, only a few problems in Scripture that I consider so thorny that I must call them errors. Fortunately all of them, as far as I can see, are unrelated to Christian faith and practice. They are such problems as how to reconcile divergent parallel accounts or statistics, how to construe apparently inaccurate chronologies, what to do with puzzling claims such as the statement that hares are ruminants (Lev. 11:6; Deut. 14:7), how to reconcile with modern science the apparent belief of some Biblical writers in a "three-story universe" (heaven above, earth in the middle, and hell below; cf. Phil. 2:10; I Thess. 4:15ff.; Rev. 5:13). As representative samples, let me mention six items that I consider to be real errors. I cannot prove that they are errors, and I will not be bothered if scholars someday show that they are not errors. All I say is that the explanations of these difficulties that I have encountered seem to me implausible. Some of the problems may seem trivial, and I agree that all are unimportant in relation to the great Biblical doctrines on which Christianity is based. But trivial or not, they do seem to me to falsify the doctrine that the Bible contains no errors.

a. The problem of the Israelite conquest. Deuteronomy and Judges make several points plain about the Israelite conquest of Canaan under Joshua. First, God gave Canaan to the Israelites; it was his will that they conquer the land (Deut. 33:27; Josh. 1:2). Second, the Israelites were successful because God fought for them (Josh. 10:8, 42). Third, it was God's will that the Israelites kill every single Canaanite—man, woman, and child (Deut. 2:31–35; 3:1–8; 7:2; Josh. 6:15–21; 8:25–26; 11:12).

> So Joshua defeated the whole land; . . . he left none remaining, but utterly destroyed all that breathed, as the LORD God of Israel commanded. (Josh. 10:40)

And fourth, God hardened the hearts of the Canaanites against the idea of making peace with Israel:

> For it was the LORD's doing to harden their hearts that they should come against Israel in battle, in order that they should be utterly destroyed, and should receive no mercy but be exterminated, as the LORD commanded Moses. (Josh. 11:20)

I speak for no one except myself, but I believe that killing innocent people is morally wrong. And killing

Canaanite civilians is to be sharply distinguished from killing Canaanite soldiers in the battles that were necessary for the Israelites to conquer the land that God had promised them. I frankly find it difficult to believe that it was God's will that every Canaanite—man, woman, and child—be slaughtered. Since the Bible clearly says that this was God's will, I must conclude that the Biblical writers in this case were mistaken. The error of confusing patriotic sentiment with God's will is a common one in human history, but it is an error nonetheless.

Can this be explained by "accommodation"? If so, it is still true that an error of some sort has been made here. Was the slaughter due to God's righteous desire to punish the depraved Canaanites (Gen. 15:16; Lev. 18:24–30; Deut. 9:4–5)? Then it seems an odd coincidence that God decided to punish the Canaanites at the precise moment when the Israelites needed land. Was the slaughter necessary to keep Israel pure by removing the temptation to adopt Canaanite religion and culture (Deut. 7:1–5; 12:30)? But The Book of Joshua exults that the conquest was successful, and subsequent Biblical history shows that the Israelites did not remain pure in their obedience to God. Have I perhaps no right to complain, since my own countrymen killed innocent civilians in Vietnam? But how is this relevant, since I disapprove of the killing of *any* innocent person—whether done by an American or anyone else—and condemn it as contrary to God's will? Does my disquiet about the Israelite conquest show that I irreverently claim to have a "higher" ethic than the Bible? Not so! I believe the slaughter of innocent people violates the moral standards of the

Bible itself (Gen. 9:6; Ex. 20:13; Luke 18:20; Rom. 13:9). I find no explanation successful and must conclude that the Israelites misunderstood God's will.

b. David's numbering of the people. There is a strange inconsistency between the two Biblical accounts of King David's census. The versions agree that the census was an evil act and a judgment on the people's sinfulness. But on other items the accounts disagree. II Samuel 24:1–2 says that God was angry with Israel and therefore incited David to count the people:

> Again the anger of the LORD was kindled against Israel, and he incited David against them, saying, "Go, number Israel and Judah." So the king said to Joab and the commanders of the army, who were with him, "Go through all the tribes of Israel, from Dan to Beersheba, and number the people, that I may know the number of the people."

But I Chron. 21:1–2 says that David counted the people because Satan induced him to do so:

> Satan stood up against Israel, and incited David to number Israel. So David said to Joab and the commanders of the army, "Go, number Israel, from Beersheba to Dan, and bring me a report, that I may know their number."

(The numbers are inconsistent too: II Sam. 24:9 lists 800,000 warriors in Israel and 500,000 in Judah, while I Chron. 21:5 lists 1,100,000 warriors in Israel and 470,000 in Judah.)

Leaving aside the puzzling question why numbering the people was an evil act, it seems at first glance clear how we can account for the inconsistency between the two texts. The Chronicler (who often acts as a "corrective" on earlier accounts of the events he records) was disturbed by the notion of God inciting David to do an evil act for which he was later punished. Therefore he attributed the incitement to Satan. But this explanation cannot satisfy the inerrantist, for it entails that at least one of the accounts is mistaken.

Perhaps the inerrantist could claim that both accounts present different aspects of the truth. Perhaps God did incite David to do the act but did so through the instrumentality of Satan, i.e., by first inciting Satan to incite David to do the act. (And it might be argued that there are places in the Bible where God seems to use Satan or other evil forces in such ways, e.g., I Sam. 16:14; I Kings 22:19–23; Job 1:6–12; 2:1–6.) But this answer seems farfetched, and even if accepted, it leaves unanswered the theological issue that apparently bothered the Chronicler: How could God punish a person for doing an act that God himself had incited him to perform?

Perhaps the inerrantist could solve the inconsistency by qualifying inerrancy once again. He could deny that inspiration corrects errors in the sources used by the inspired Biblical writers. Thus it might be said of this difficulty that inspiration merely guaranteed that Kings and Chronicles inerrantly reproduced the different accounts of the census which the authors of these works used as sources. The sources available to the author of Kings named God as the instigator of the census and the sources used by the Chronicler named Satan. But this seems a singularly dangerous avenue of escape for the inerrantist. A person could both believe in inerrancy and deny anything at all that the Bible says (even, say, the creation of the world by God or the death of Jesus on the cross) on the grounds that the Biblical writers (in Genesis and in the Gospels) merely inerrantly reproduced what their sources (errantly) affirmed.

I see no satisfactory solution to this difficulty and conclude that the accounts of the census in Kings and Chronicles are indeed inconsistent.

c. The "mustard seed" problem. In Matt. 13:31–32 Jesus says:

> The kingdom of heaven is like a grain of mustard seed which a man took and sowed in his field; it is the smallest of all seeds, but when it has grown it is the greatest of shrubs and becomes a tree, so that the birds of the air come and make nests in its branches.

And this is in error, because botanists know of seeds that are smaller than the mustard seed. Some orchid seeds, for example, are smaller. Accordingly, this looks to be a simple scientific error.

As we have seen, Fuller and others try to solve the problem by appealing to Jesus' intent. Lindsell too takes this line. He says:

> The *American Commentary* says of this passage that it was popular language [Lindsell means that the mustard seed was proverbial in Palestine for its smallness, and this is true. Cf. Matt. 17:20], and it was the intention of the speaker to communicate the fact that the mustard seed was "the smallest that his hearers were accustomed to sow." And indeed this may well be the case. In that event there was no error. If the critics of Scripture wish to use the intention of the writer, this is one place it can be used in favor of inerrancy.[51]

Jesus' main point is indeed theological and not botanical. Nevertheless, he surely did intend to say that the "mustard seed . . . is the smallest of all seeds." So at least some sort of error is being made, although perhaps not an error regarding the main point of the passage.

Lindsell next says:

> Matthew Henry in his commentary has it read, the mustard seed "which is one of the least of all seeds." From the Greek it is not clear that Jesus was saying that the mustard seed is the smallest of all the seeds on the earth. He was saying it is less than all the seeds. What must be determined is what the words "all the seeds" mean here. If Jesus was talking about the seeds commonly known to the people of that day, the affect of his word was different from what they would have been if he was speaking of all the seeds on the earth.[52]

Matthew's phrase is saying, "which is indeed less than all the seeds." Henry's account is a possible but in my opinion improbable interpretation of Matthew. It is obviously a rendering influenced by the "mustard seed" problem. We can be sure no such interpretation would ever have been suggested were it in fact true that the mustard seed is the smallest of all seeds. But this "solution" ignores Mark's parallel account (Mark 4:31), which makes explicit what Jesus meant: "less than all the seeds that are on the earth." Here, as often occurs, Matthew has retained Mark's meaning while condensing his account. In the light of Mark's explicit reference to "all the seeds on earth," the interpretation of Jesus' words on which Henry and Lindsell base their solution to the mustard seed problem appears quite unjustified.

Clark Pinnock[53] correctly points out that the Greek word used here for "small" is comparative rather than superlative in form ("smaller," not "smallest"). But this does not help. It is typical in Koine Greek to use the comparative form as a superlative, and this is clearly one such case. Of course this is not just typical of Koine Greek, but of many other languages as well —including English. The expressions, "Jones is the world's fast*est* human" and "Jones is fast*er* than any other human in the world" are virtually identical in meaning.

d. Matthew's quotation of Jeremiah. Matthew 27: 9–10 says:

> Then was fulfilled what had been spoken by the prophet Jeremiah, saying, "And they took the thirty pieces of silver, the price of him on whom a price had been set by some of the sons of Israel, and they gave them for the potter's field, as the Lord directed me."

The difficulty here is that the quoted words are found nowhere in Jeremiah. In fact, the passage is most probably a loose quotation, perhaps from memory, of Zech. 11:12–13:

> Then I said to them, "If it seems right to you, give me my wages; but if not, keep them." And they weighed out as my wages thirty shekels of silver. Then the LORD said to me, "Cast it into the treasury"—the lordly price at which I was paid off by them. So I took the thirty shekels of silver and cast them into the treasury in the house of the LORD.

"Into the treasury" could be and sometimes is translated "to the potter." Apparently the Evangelist sees in Zechariah's throwing his wages to the potter a fore-shadowing of the high priest's using Judas' wages to buy the potter's field.

A good many suggestions have been made concerning this apparent error on the part of the Gospel writer. Since the precise words he quotes are found nowhere in the Old Testament, some suggest they may have come from a lost work of Jeremiah or from a saying of his which was preserved only orally. This could be true, but seems improbable. Others suggest that Matthew is indeed alluding to events of The Book of Jeremiah, and his quotation does have some vague parallels with Jer. 18:2–3; 19:1, 11; and 32:6–15. But this also seems improbable. Zechariah 11:12–13 appears to be a much better candidate for the text that the Evangelist has in mind. In any case, it leaves unanswered the question of precisely where Jeremiah makes the prophecy the Gospel writer thinks is fulfilled by the events surrounding the death of Judas.

Others point out that Jeremiah and Zechariah were associated with each other in Jewish tradition and that Jeremiah was regarded as the head of the prophets and was so named in the Babylonian Talmud. But even if this is so, it still seems to be an error of some sort to name Jeremiah as the source of a prophecy that actually came from Zechariah. And if the Evangelist did indeed have in mind the entire prophetic section of the Old Testament of which Jeremiah was commonly regarded as the head, why does he so commonly cite prophets other than Jeremiah elsewhere in his Gospel? Finally, some suggest an early scribal error in the text of Matthew. Indeed, the words "spoken by the prophet" rather than "spoken by the prophet Jere-

miah" appear in some manuscripts. But this variant is
poorly attested, leaving me, at least, with no probable
solution to this difficulty.

   e. The "Enoch" problem. Enoch was an Old Testament patriarch who was the son of Jared and the father
of Methuselah. He "walked with God" and was
"taken" by God at age 365 (see Gen. 5:18–24; I
Chron. 1:3; Luke 3:37; Heb. 11:5). In Jude, the penul-
timate book of the Bible, we find the following words:

> It was of these also that Enoch in the seventh genera-
> tion from Adam prophesied, saying, "Behold, the
> Lord came with his holy myriads, to execute judgment
> on all, and to convict all the ungodly of all their deeds
> of ungodliness which they have committed in such an
> ungodly way, and of all the harsh things which un-
> godly sinners have spoken against him." (Jude 14–15)

Jude seems to believe he is quoting the patriarch
Enoch ("the seventh generation from Adam"), but
the words he attributes to Enoch actually come from
the pseudepigraphal Book of Enoch, an apocalyptic
book that was probably written in the first century B.C.
"Pseudepigraphal" means that the author attributes
the book not to himself but to a well-known Biblical
character, perhaps to give the work added impact and
authority. This book was known to Jews and Christians
of the first and second centuries A.D., and its non-
canonical status was not finally settled until later.

   It seems clear, then, that an error has been made
here. Jude thinks the patriarch Enoch spoke the words
he quotes, when they were actually written by the
unknown author of the Book of Enoch (they are found
in Enoch 1:9). I doubt that there was any intention to
deceive. Jude probably shared the common first-cen-

tury belief that the patriarch Enoch wrote the Book of Enoch. I suppose a defender of inerrancy could claim that the patriarch Enoch really did speak these words, but this seems a desperate expedient, as Carnell points out. "Of course, Orthodoxy can always say that Jude knew by inspiration that the seventh from Adam spoke the words that now appear in the book of Enoch; but the explanation sounds suspiciously affected."[54] Other explanations have been suggested, but all seem implausible, at least to me. The notion that through Jude the Holy Spirit was merely accommodating himself to common ignorance still ends up with an error, one of perhaps a different sort—an intended error—but an error nevertheless. If one appeals to the overall intent of Jude in the passage ("not to quote the patriarch but to condemn ungodliness"), the same can be said. The proper conclusion, I feel, is that here an error has been made.

f. The "staff" problem. There is a curious divergence between Matthew and Luke, on the one hand, and Mark, on the other, in their accounts of the instructions Jesus gave to the disciples before sending them on a preaching mission. Mark has Jesus allow the taking of a staff:

> He charged them to take nothing for their journey except a staff; no bread, no bag, no money in their belts. (Mark 6:8)

But Matthew and Luke have Jesus specifically prohibiting the taking of a staff:

> Take no gold, nor silver, nor copper in your belts, no bag for your journey, nor two tunics, nor sandals, nor a staff. (Matt. 10:9–10)

> Take nothing for your journey, no staff, nor bag, nor
> bread, nor money. (Luke 9:3)

I know of no way to reconcile this inconsistency. Each
account can be interpreted as making sense in the
context of the disciples' mission, and the text of each
passage is well attested. Harrison says that the unusual
situation of Matthew and Luke agreeing with each
other over against Mark might make us conjecture that
there was an early alteration in the text of Mark. But
he recognizes that "speculation cannot do much to
resolve the riddle."[55] I agree with this. The proper
conclusion, I think, is that the accounts are inconsistent
and that at least one of the Gospels is in error.

It appears, then, that there are indeed what can be
called errors in Scripture. Fortunately, all the ones I
know of are unimportant and unrelated to anything I
would consider Christian faith and practice. I do not
claim that these problems and others like them cannot
be solved. I do not begin with an *a priori* assumption
that the Bible must be errant. I just claim that the
solutions that have been suggested do not seem satisfactory to me. Some inerrantists insist that phenomenological difficulties in the Bible ought to count little
when placed against the Biblical argument for inerrancy,[56] but Everett Harrison's comment seems wiser.
Speaking of the phenomenological difficulties that
seem to rule out inerrancy, he says: "If the inductive
study of the Bible reveals enough examples of this sort
of thing to make the conclusion probable, then we
shall have to hold the doctrine of inspiration in this
light. We may have our own ideas as to how God
should have inspired the Word, but it is more profit-

able to learn, if we can, how he has actually inspired it."[57]

THE NOTION OF INTENT

2. The device of appealing to the intention of the Biblical writer, which is used by virtually every contemporary defender of inerrancy, raises more problems than it solves. As we have seen, appealing to the intent of the Biblical writer, which is alleged not to be mistaken, is a device used by many inerrantists to defend their doctrine against phenomenological difficulties. I agree that looking for the intended meaning of the author is a sound hermeneutical principle: in interpreting Scripture, we ought to look for the plain sense or literal meaning of the passage, i.e., to what the author intended to convey. But as a way of rescuing inerrancy, the device is problematical, as we have seen in Chapter 1. As I said there, we need actually to speak not of the *intention* of the writer in a passage but rather of the *main point he was making.* Even so, it seems that this does not save the Bible from error. Even if Jesus' main point in Matt. 13:31–32 is theological rather than botanical, and even if his mustard seed simile *perfectly* illustrates his point, it still seems to be some sort of error to say that the mustard seed is the smallest of all seeds. Defenders of inerrancy can always deny that this is the sort of "error" they have in mind when they claim that the Bible is inerrant. But as I noted earlier, Jesus certainly did intentionally make the offending remark, no doubt as an attempt to give a good *and true* illustration of his theological point. So some part of his intention seems to have failed. Al-

though the illustration of his point is appropriate and clear, it is not factually true.

Another difficulty looms. Suppose the inerrantist says that what he is protecting is the doctrine that the main point being made in every passage or text in the Bible is correct. Then the obvious next question is, How do we determine the limits of a "passage" or "text"? Is a passage a testament? a book? a chapter? an RSV paragraph? a verse? a form criticism pericope? or what? This is not a quibble, but a relevant concern. It may well be that such sentences as "The mustard seed . . . is the smallest of all seeds" (Matt. 13:32a), or "After [Abraham's] father died, God removed him from [Haran] into this land in which you are now living" (Acts 7:4b) constitute actual Biblical passages or texts. (Again, the problem with Acts 7:4b is that it seems to contradict Gen. 11:26, 32; 12:4, which indicate that Abraham left for Canaan sixty years before his father, Terah, died.) And if so, the main points being made in *these* passages, if not in their larger contexts, are false, and the doctrine that the inerrantist says he is defending is false. We can see from this that the "intent" criterion does not save inerrancy. Or, at the very least, it needs to be much more precisely defined.

I cannot help feeling that there is a slight air of dishonesty, undoubtedly unintended, about appeals to intent and other machinations of inerrantists. Somehow it seems "slippery" to classify a serious phenomenological problem as a "yet to be resolved difficulty" rather than a contradiction or error. In the same way it seems slippery to claim, as Lindsell does, that the Bible "does not contain error of any kind," then to qualify this definition in the light of phenomenal problems by saying, "The Bible contains no *intended* error," and still end up boldly affirming that the Bible is inerrant.

I do not dispute the right to hold to a position despite admitted difficulties. Presumably there are difficulties for *all* positions on all theological subjects. What one should do, I suppose, is adopt the position that is beset with the least difficulties. But defenders of inerrancy sometimes argue in this vaguely inconsistent way. First they say something like this: "We wouldn't think much of Jesus if he had said some false things along with a lot of true things. We have the high regard for him that we do in part because everything he says is true." But then when confronted with a phenomenological problem they resort to the notion of intent or offer some other qualification so that they can still insist that the Bible is inerrant, *despite containing some errors.*

BUSY AT THE WRONG TASKS

3. Inerrancy emphasizes the wrong tasks. It leads to defending obscure minutiae in Scripture rather than proclaiming its message. This argument and the next are not exactly arguments against the truth of the claim that the Bible is inerrant. I see them as objectionable aspects of the way inerrancy is typically defended.

This point regarding tasks arises from a feeling on my part that defending the truth of obscure Biblical texts is not the best way for Christians to spend their time. Inerrantists feel inclined to do this under the influence of the epistemological argument: "If Scripture is wrong anywhere, the whole edifice of Christianity collapses." But this argument is unconvincing. Personally I believe that the Bible is amazingly accurate and trustworthy on all matters, which is one reason I regard it as the word of God, and not just a human book. The large freedom from factual error that we see in Scripture is one of its most impressive qualities. But it is certainly not its only impressive quality. Frankly I think that *I* could write an inerrant book—even by the unqualified definition of "inerrant." It would be a book in which I would be careful to make only factual claims that are obviously true, and otherwise scrupulously avoid making any factual claims at all. (Perhaps it would be a novel, or a book of poetry that contained no declarative statements.) But even if I could write such a book, I know one thing about it: it would not inspire, teach, guide, convict, and empower as the Bible does. Nor would it constitute a revelation from God that grips people at the deepest level of their being, as the Bible does. It is this quality of the Bible that we must stress: how its message speaks redemptively to the concrete needs of men and women. Explaining this is what evangelical scholars ought to be doing, not trying desperately to prove that donkeys can talk (Num. 22:30), that there were really six Petrine denials, or that Isaiah's reference to "the circle of the earth" (Isa. 40:22) shows he knew that the earth is round.

A Defensive Doctrine

4. Inerrancy appears to make all of Christianity hang upon the successful completion of this "defending"

enterprise. There is no doubt that the heavy use of the epistemological argument and the slippery slide argument by defenders of inerrancy at least *gives the impression* that one proven error in one obscure passage of the Bible pulls down with it the reliability of the whole Bible and thus Christianity. This appears to be a suicidal position, as James Orr, a turn-of-the-century evangelical who did not believe in inerrancy, points out:

> It is urged, e.g., that unless we can demonstrate what is called the "inerrancy" of the Biblical record, down even to its minutest details, the whole edifice of belief in revealed religion falls to the ground. This, on the face of it, is a most suicidal position for any defender of revelation to take up.[58]

This all-or-nothing mentality is satirized by the following bit of nineteenth-century doggerel, which refers to the claim that hares are ruminants:

> The bishops all have sworn to shed their blood
> To prove 'tis true the hare doth chew the cud.
> O' bishops, doctors, and divines, beware—
> Weak is the faith that hangs upon a hare.[59]

Lindsell recognizes the seriousness of the matter, and insists that the position Orr calls "suicidal" is not his own. He denies that he would give up the Christian faith in its entirety if an error were found in the Bible, nor, he says, would any other believer in inerrancy that he knows.[60] This makes good sense and I am glad to hear that Lindsell is not espousing the suicidal position. But whether or not inerrantists actually do espouse this position, they certainly give the impression that they do, and it appears to follow from the logic of at least some of their statements. For example, consider these two statements from *The Battle for the Bible:*

> The presence of one error invalidates the claim to biblical inerrancy.

> When inerrancy goes, it opens a small hole in the dike, and if that hole is not closed, the levee will collapse and the whole land will be overrun with the waters of unbelief not unlike that exhibited by Bultmann and theological liberalism.[61]

If Lindsell and other defenders of inerrancy really do not mean to be defending the view that one Biblical error brings with it the demise of the orthodox Christian position, they should stop talking as if this is what they mean. They had best give up using the epistemological argument and the slippery slide argument, which are the arguments primarily responsible for this apparently mistaken impression. One further comment is in order. Inerrantists do seem passionately committed to the project of rescuing the Bible from every alleged error. This too creates the impression which Lindsell says is mistaken. It seems *in practice* that inerrantists feel impelled to defend every seeming error, every seeming inconsistency, every seeming immoral injunction in the Bible. Whatever the inerrantists' position (and perhaps as a minimum we should ask them to clarify it), my own position does not require that I participate in this project of defending every statement that is made in the Bible. Not having that weight on my shoulders is to me liberating.

It can now be seen why I do not find inerrancy a defensible doctrine. (1) The Bible does not teach inerrancy. (2) The phenomena do not demand inerrancy and in fact seem to require the opposite. Inerrancy only seems possible after all sorts of implausible terminological, exegetical, and apologetic handstands are turned. (3) None of the philosophical arguments for inerrancy seem successful. And (4) the doctrine is open to several serious difficulties.

So why should we believe in inerrancy? Why should we believe that inerrancy is crucial to the Christian position? Why should we believe that those who deny inerrancy are not true evangelicals?

6

INFALLIBILITY

So far I have mainly criticized the doctrine of inerrancy. Nowhere have I attempted to construct my own systematic doctrine of Scripture. I have said very little about such crucial concepts as the Bible canon, revelation, inspiration, Biblical criticism, and hermeneutics. I hope that someday someone will construct a full-blown, non-inerrant, evangelical doctrine of Scripture. I am not the one to do so; it is a task that should be left for systematic theologians. Nevertheless, I believe the broad outlines of my attitude toward the Bible are clear by now. Since the remarks that reveal this attitude are scattered throughout the book, perhaps I ought to bring them together so that the doctrine which I regard as superior to inerrancy can be clearly grasped. This will be the first task of this chapter. Since my theory will perhaps be classified as a species of "limited inerrancy," I wish also to say something in response to criticisms that inerrantists bring against limited inerrancy.

INFALLIBLE BUT NOT INERRANT

1. I regard the Bible as the word of God. I do not regard it merely as *containing* the word of God or as

a *witness* to how God has revealed himself in the past, although this is part of what the Bible does. Nor do I say that the Bible becomes the word of God only when certain conditions are met—e.g., when it speaks in an illuminating way to a given person. The Bible not only tells how God has revealed himself in the past; it also authoritatively interprets for us the meaning of these events. Thus the Bible in itself, and not just as a witness to past revelatory events, constitutes a revelation of God's nature, will, and purpose. God speaks to us in the Bible; it is our divine teacher on all matters of faith and practice. It is the word of God.

2. But it is also the words of human beings. God reveals himself in the Bible through the instrumentality of its human authors. The Biblical writers wrote in various historical, cultural, and theological contexts, and each author's distinctive style and concerns are evident. This rules out any mechanical dictation theory of inspiration. But I do believe in the inspiration of the writers of the Bible. In my opinion, this makes the Bible unique among all the books that have ever been written. The Holy Spirit so influenced these writers that what they wrote was an authoritative and trustworthy account of God's revelatory acts in history and the authoritative theological interpretation of these acts. Both the account and the interpretation are therefore revelatory. God has revealed himself in both deeds and words, and the Bible is the record of both modes of revelation.[62]

3. The Bible is infallible, as I define that term, but not inerrant. That is, there are historical and scientific errors in the Bible, but I have found none on matters of faith and practice. I do not claim *a priori* that the

Bible is or must be infallible, just that I have found it
to be so. Perhaps someday it will be shown that the
Bible is not infallible. For now I can only affirm infallibility as the most probable interpretation of the evidence I see. The Bible is amazingly accurate even on
obscure historical matters—as modern scholarship and
archaeology have increasingly discovered. But there
are some items I must at present regard as errors. My
willingness to affirm that the Bible is infallible does not
mean that I claim to understand everything that the
Bible says that is relevant to Christian faith and practice. There are difficulties for the person who holds
that the Bible is infallible, which I freely admit. Paul's
apparent sexism is one; the relationship between election and freedom of choice is another; Jesus' apparent
belief that the Parousia would occur within the life-
times of some of those who were listening to him is
another. It should be noted that I have said nothing
about *autographs.* These manuscripts play no particular
role in my understanding of the Bible. I believe that
presently existing Bibles are infallible works that constitute the word of God for all who read them.

4. I believe that the Bible is or ought to be authoritative for every Christian in all that it says on any subject
unless and until he encounters a passage which after
careful study and for good reasons he cannot accept.
The Bible is and ought to be the source of all Christian
thinking and doing. A doctrine is to be accepted by
Christians if and only if it is either explicitly taught in
the Bible, or is either presupposed or implied by what
is explicitly taught in the Bible. I know of few persons
who are prepared to admit that they have a warrant to

believe irrational claims, and so it is apparent that reason has a critical function to play in *all* beliefs, religious as well as nonreligious. Reason must help determine what the Bible says and, ultimately, whether or not what it says is acceptable. Those who deny that this is their procedure, I argue, are only fooling themselves.[63]

5. I believe that the historical-critical study of the Bible ought to be welcomed and encouraged by evangelicals. Any method or discipline that helps us understand God's word, and thus helps it speak to us with greater clarity, is desirable. There are philosophical assumptions that some Biblical critics make about the Bible—e.g., that supernatural events such as resurrections and other miracles are just not the sorts of things that happen—that lead them to conclusions unacceptable to evangelicals. These assumptions and conclusions ought to be resisted. Furthermore, the *exclusive* concern with critical issues in many of today's graduate schools of religion seems to me to have produced a whole cadre of technically skilled Biblical scholars who seem unable or unwilling to let the Bible speak to modern men and women on the issues to which it addresses itself.[64] But none of this seems to me to condemn the scientific study of the Bible in itself—just the way this study is sometimes carried out.

6. Finally, a few further comments about the word "infallible" are perhaps in order. Normally this term is synonymous with the word "inerrant," but I have offered my own technical definitions and have not used these two terms synonymously. Thus it would not be true to say that Biblical infallibility, as I understand

this concept, is so close in meaning to Biblical inerrancy as to be virtually indistinguishable from it. The person who affirms infallibility does not necessarily believe that every statement made by the Biblical writers is true, nor does he feel any need to write books or articles defending everything the Bible says.

Nevertheless, my notion of Biblical infallibility remains a high view of the Bible that affirms, in my opinion, all that evangelicals need to affirm about the Scriptures. This notion says that the Bible is fully trustworthy and never misleads us on matters that are crucially relevant to Christian faith and practice. I say "crucially relevant" because "relevant" would be too broad. In some sense, probably everything in the Bible is "relevant to" everything else, just as every event or thing in the universe is probably somehow related to everything else on the continuum of cause and effect. Thus the claim in II Sam. 21:19 that Elhanan killed Goliath (and not David, as is claimed elsewhere) is probably somehow relevant to Paul's teachings on justification by faith. But surely it is not crucially relevant. The truth of Paul's doctrine does not depend on the resolution of this historical difficulty, nor in my opinion does any other item of Christian faith and practice.

Why not drop the term "infallible" altogether? It is not a Biblical term and has the disadvantage of being negative. Perhaps a better, more positive Biblical term can be found. Possibly so, but for now I wish to retain this word because I can think of no better one and because I do indeed believe that the Bible is infallible, as I define the word. Again, I do not make this affirmation as a philosophical *a priori:* it just seems to be an adjective that aptly fits the Bible we read. Further-more, as G. C. Berkouwer[65] points out, to abandon the term would be too severe a break with the long-standing Christian tradition that the Bible is a God-breathed revelation, as if there were now some reason for us no longer to affirm this. And finally, as Clark Pinnock is fond of saying, we need a strong term like "infallible" in order sharply to distinguish evangelical from nonevangelical views of the Bible. We do not agree with those who say that the Bible merely con-tains the word of God, or merely testifies to past acts of divine revelation. We have even less in common with those who view the Bible as an interesting, influ-ential, beautiful, lofty, but entirely human book.

The term "infallible" will be unacceptable to some. Whatever term is adopted, I wish to ally myself with a view of the Bible that posits its full doctrinal and moral teaching authority over the church, but which avoids the mentality of inerrancy. That is, it avoids the mentality that feels a need to prove that everything the Bible says is correct, that thinks this defending enter-prise is somehow crucial to Christianity, and that ostra-cizes those who do not share enthusiasm for this pro-ject.

One final matter in this regard. It might be asked whether my doctrine of Biblical infallibility provides as solid a way of assuring the truth of the major Chris-tian doctrines as Biblical inerrancy is designed to do. In one sense the answer to this is yes, for if I am correct that the Bible is infallible, then if a given doctrine can be shown both to be taught in the Bible and to be crucially relevant to Christian faith and practice, that doctrine is true. But in another sense the answer is no, for I affirm Biblical infallibility not as a theological *a priori*—i.e., because the doctrine is needed for some theological or apologetic reason—but simply because this seems to be a good way to describe the Bible. The Bible I read just does seem to me infallible, as I define the term. But I am open at any point to the possibility that the Bible is not infallible. Perhaps some future argument or discovery will ruin my doctrine of Biblical infallibility. I hope this does not happen, but I agree with Fuller that induction requires leaving the possibility open. Thus, whatever "epistemological basis" infallibility provides for other doctrines is contingent upon our continued ability rationally to maintain that the Bible is infallible.

RESPONSES TO CRITICS OF LIMITED INERRANCY

My theory will probably be classified by some as a species of "limited inerrancy." I do not like this contradictory term, nor do I wish it to apply to my views. I prefer to say that I do not believe in inerrancy at all. Nevertheless, I will now address myself to some criticisms of limited inerrancy that have been made by John W. Montgomery and others, for these criticisms are quite possibly relevant to my theory.

First, Montgomery argues that all human knowledge on all subjects is interrelated and is ultimately one. His first criticism of any limit on inerrancy is based on this claim. He sums it up in this way:

> For practical purposes we may—perhaps we must—distinguish between "historical," "geographical," and "theological" statements in Holy Writ; but these dis-

tinctions are no more inherent to reality than the divisions between hands and wrist or trunk and branches. It is thus logically impossible to argue for an alleged perfection resident "spiritually" in Scripture while admitting imperfections in scriptural knowledge viewed from a "secular" standpoint. Fallibility in the latter necessitates fallibility in the former—and this leaves one incapable of affirming a single doctrinal or moral teaching of the Bible with finality.[66]

This is a difficult argument to construe precisely, and it is difficult to see how it is relevant to my own view, since I make no distinction between "sacred" and "secular" or "spiritual" and "nonspiritual" content in Scripture. Perhaps Montgomery would claim that my distinction between matters of faith and practice and other matters *amounts to* something like this distinction. Perhaps this would be correct. But it is still not easy to catch the drift of his argument. Montgomery appears to be arguing as follows:

1. All knowledge is ultimately one.

2. Therefore, no distinction between true and false Biblical claims can be made.

This argument is clearly relevant to my theory. I want to deny 2, but unfortunately it is obviously and blatantly invalid. What possibly is valid is this argument:

1. All knowledge is ultimately one.

3. Therefore, no distinction between true and false Biblical *knowledge* can be made.

But I am not interested in affirming 3: It is surely true that whatever *knowledge* there is in the Bible is not false. A false proposition—such as "Kissinger antedates Caesar"—cannot be *known.* What I want to affirm is that some statements in the Bible are false and thus *are not known,* and it is hard to see how Montgomery's first argument casts doubt on this.

Incidentally, I agree with Montgomery's implicit claim about the unity of the Bible's message. I believe that the whole Bible contains one message: from beginning to end it is about Jesus Christ and God's redemptive victory over sin and death through him. But, obviously, distinctions among various Biblical claims can be made for various purposes. To illustrate this, let me ask two questions: Can a person be a Christian and not believe in the resurrection of Jesus Christ from the dead? and, Can a person be a Christian and not believe that Joshua made the sun stand still (Josh. 10:12–14)? I would say no to the first question and yes to the second, and I suspect that most Christians would agree with me. This shows, I think, that even if the Bible preaches one message from beginning to end, we can still distinguish between Biblical claims that are crucial and those that are not.

Secondly, Montgomery also argues that limited inerrancy ends up denying the incarnation of Christ.[67] His argument appears to run as follows:

4. Jesus believed that the Bible is inerrant.

5. The Bible is not inerrant.

6. Therefore, Jesus is not the incarnate son of God.

Again, this argument needs to be amended; as it stands it is formally invalid. It appears to become formally valid if we add:

5a. Jesus believed a falsehood.

and

5b. No person who believes a falsehood is the incarnate son of God.

We now have a valid argument, but is it sound? I do not believe so. In the first place, I deny that anyone knows that 4 is true. Jesus did apparently regard the Old Testament as inspired, authoritative, and reliable in its details, but I can find nowhere in the Gospels any teaching by Jesus that states, implies, or presupposes 4. Furthermore, for obvious reasons, Jesus nowhere says a single word about any of the books that now form the New Testament.

I have doubts about 5b as well, although it would involve too extended an excursus into Christology to argue the point convincingly. Paul says that in the incarnation Jesus "did not count equality with God a thing to be grasped, but emptied himself, taking the form of a servant, being born in the likeness of men" (Phil. 2:6–7). One traditional way of interpreting these words is to say that in the incarnation Jesus gave up some of his divine attributes, one of which is omniscience. Indeed we know from his own lips that Jesus was not omniscient, for when asked when the Parousia and the other events of the last days would occur, he replied, "But of that day and hour no one knows, not even the angels of heaven, nor the Son, but the Father only" (Matt. 24:36). This shows that Jesus was not omniscient, but it does not necessarily show that he had false beliefs. But if he really "emptied himself" and became "truly man," as ancient creeds affirm, then perhaps he shared with the people of his day certain false beliefs. Perhaps he believed that the earth is flat I do not know whether or not Jesus believed this, because the Gospels do not record his opinion on the subject. And not being a systematic theologian by trade, I confess I have not thought through all the implications of the different possibilities here. But if Jesus did hold certain false beliefs in common with the people of his day, I do not see how this contradicts the equally ancient affirmation that he was also "truly God." Matthew 24:36 certainly does not contradict this—at least I know of no one who says it does. Possibly I am mistaken. Perhaps some theologian can show that Jesus could not have held false beliefs. I don't know how this could be proved, however, so it certainly seems possible that 5b is false; and if it is, Montgomery's second argument is unsuccessful.

Finally, I wish to answer an objection to "limited inerrancy" that is implicit in Montgomery's article and is urged by many other critics. It is this: If limited inerrancy is true, how can we successfully distinguish between those Biblical claims that are true and those that are false? Or, to put it in terms equally relevant for my theory: How can we successfully distinguish between Biblical claims that are crucially relevant to Christian faith and practice and those that are not?

I have no hard-and-fast answer to this question. I suspect there is something of a consensus on the category to which most Biblical items belong. For example, I think most persons would agree that the claim that Jesus rose from the dead is a matter of faith and practice and the claim that there were several other giants besides Goliath in the army of the Philistines (II Sam. 21:15–22; I Chron. 20:4–8) is not. Fuller is quite right in saying that some historical events (such as the resurrection and the exodus) are intimately tied to matters of faith and practice, and if Biblical claims that these events occurred are false, then the Bible is not infallible. What we must do in these cases, as in all cases, is examine what the Bible says in the light of the available evidence and see whether or not there is reason to doubt it. My own view is that the evidence decisively favors the opinion that these events did occur as claimed.

Nevertheless, I admit that I am unable to stipulate a clear and infallible criterion to distinguish Biblical passages that are crucially relevant to faith and practice from those that are not. This would be a serious difficulty for my theory if the epistemological argument were sound. It would then follow that we have not one sure word from God on matters of faith and practice, since we are unable to say for sure where the Bible speaks on matters of faith and practice. But, as we have seen, the epistemological argument is not sound, and so my inability to stipulate the requested criterion is not so serious after all. Ultimately, such decisions must be made by careful exegesis and theology. If these disciplines show that a given Biblical text is crucially relevant to faith and practice, then it must be regarded as such. If this is not shown, it need not be regarded as a matter of faith and practice.

I should reiterate that my affirmation of Biblical infallibility means simply that I find no errors in the Bible that are crucially relevant to Christian faith and practice. It does not necessarily mean that I find no *theological error* in the Bible as opposed, say, to scientific or historical error. For example, as we have seen,

the Bible claims that the slaughter of Canaanite inno-
cents was the will of God, and I claim that this could
not have been God's will. Is this, then, a theological
or a historical error in the Bible? "Theological" is a
hard word to define, but even if it is indeed a theological error, it will not refute my notion of Biblical infallibility. For I see nothing here that is crucially relevant
to Christian faith and practice. As I do exegesis and
theology, no point of Christian faith and practice
seems to me to hinge on the Bible's being correct at
this point.

"GOOD" REASONS TO CHALLENGE BIBLICAL CLAIMS

A related difficulty might be raised about my view
of the Bible. I claim that all that the Bible says ought
to be authoritative for the evangelical Christian unless
after careful study he finds good reason to reject some
Biblical claim. It might be objected that the notion of
"good reason" is far from clear. How can one tell
what counts as a good reason and what does not? Is not
this standard far too permissive? Anyone can come
along and claim he has a good reason to reject anything in the Bible—even its most central claims. Does
this not leave room for introducing all sorts of attitudes toward the Bible that are unacceptable to evangelicals, e.g., the attitude of accepting whatever in the
Bible one likes and rejecting whatever one dislikes?

It is quite true that the notion of "good reason" is
imprecise and flexible. It does not constitute an infallible criterion for what is and is not to be accepted in
Scripture. This much I admit. But I see no reason to

believe that my notion introduces unbelieving attitudes toward the Bible. Concretely what must be done is this: If a person rejects a given Biblical claim on the basis of reasons a, b, and c, these reasons must be investigated by patient, thorough exegesis and theology. These reasons are indeed "good" reasons if the weight of available evidence supports the conclusion that on the basis of a, b, and c the Biblical claim in question is to be rejected.

As noted earlier, I personally find it difficult to accept the Biblical claim that it was God's will for the Israelites under Joshua to kill every single Canaanite. I reject this claim, because the available evidence leads me to do so. Perhaps I am mistaken. Perhaps future exegesis and theology will show that my reasons are not good reasons. If this happens, my position will be shown to be in error. I welcome any attempt to show that my reasons are not convincing. But until this is done, I believe I have the epistemological right to hold the position that I hold.

But this is a far cry from a person's rejecting a Biblical claim merely because he disagrees with it or dislikes it, or, without investigation, assumes that it is mistaken. Just because someone rejects something in the Bible does not necessarily mean that he does so for good reasons. We have to ask *why* he rejects it. A person can *claim* to have good reasons to reject a Biblical statement without in fact having good reasons; investigation might show his reasons to be weak. But, equally, if someone rejects a given Biblical claim because on investigation the weight of evidence opposes it and there are no nonfoolish ways of overcoming this evidence, this will then constitute "good reason."

This explanation may leave some people dis-
satisfied. So I wish further to point out that the ambiguity of what constitutes a "good reason" is not a
difficulty that attaches just to my view of the authority
of the Bible. It seems to me, in fact, that exactly analogous difficulties plague all the current inerrancy theories. Such difficulties will attach to any but the most
rigid and doctrinaire inerrancy doctrine, by which I
mean one that qualifies its claim that the Bible is inerrant in none of the ways I listed in Chapter 1 and in
no other way either. I know of no defender of inerrancy who holds such an unqualified doctrine. The
reason the present problem holds for all qualified inerrancy doctrines is that there are cases where it is far
from obvious whether or not the stipulated qualifications hold.

For example, suppose a given inerrantist holds the
following qualified doctrine: All statements in the
Bible are true that correspond to the *intention* of the
Biblical writer in the passage in question. Or: All statements in the Bible are true that constitute actual *claims*
or *affirmations* made by the Bible. Then the question
must be asked: How can we be sure in the case of any
Biblical statement whether or not it corresponds to the
intention of the Biblical writer or constitutes an actual
Biblical claim or affirmation? Since disputes can obviously arise over such issues (hermeneutics is not an
exact science), some criterion not unlike my own must
be appealed to: A statement will correspond to the
intention of the Biblical writer or will constitute a
Biblical claim if there is, on investigation, *good reason*
to hold that this is so. Since there is no infallible criterion for determining what the intent of a writer in a

passage is, or what actual claims or affirmations are made in the Bible, the inerrantist who qualifies his doctrine in some such way as this (and all the inerrantists that I know of do so) is equally open to the objection that might be raised against my view.

I do not claim that my view of the authority of the Bible is immune to all criticism. What I do claim is that none of the objections discussed in this chapter refutes it and that it is a far more defensible position than inerrancy.

7

IMPLICATIONS

LET ME INTRODUCE a distinction between two sorts of people who believe in inerrancy. There are those whom I will call "divisive inerrantists" and those whom I will call "nondivisive inerrantists." Divisive inerrantists are those who (1) believe in inerrancy and (2) believe that a person cannot be considered an evangelical Christian unless he believes in inerrancy. Nondivisive inerrantists are those of whom 1 but not 2 is true. I have no particular quarrel with nondivisive inerrantists. I disagree with their doctrine but applaud their attitude. But it is difficult for me to understand the divisive inerrantists. One wonders what is to be gained from taking the position they hold.

The thought of no longer being called an "evangelical" is not an alarming prospect. I happen to like the term and would prefer to be free to continue to call myself an evangelical, but the name is not what ultimately counts. What I do find troubling are the practical implications of divisive inerrancy. Suppose the divisive inerrantists win out and people like me can no longer be considered evangelicals—what will this mean pragmatically? Will it mean that non-inerrantist professors can no longer be hired by certain under-graduate and theological faculties? Will it mean that non-inerrantist editors will be fired from editorial boards of religious publications? Will it mean that the works of non-inerrantist Christian writers will not be published? Will it mean that non-inerrantist missionaries will be asked by their home agencies to give up their work and return home? Will it mean that non-inerrantist seminary graduates will be refused ordination? Will it mean that non-inerrantist ministers will be tried for heresy? I do not know the answers to these questions; I am not sure precisely what the divisive inerrantists mean to suggest. But the prospects are horrifying. So these are two questions that must be asked of such people: What actually do you mean when you say that people who do not affirm that the Bible is inerrant are not true evangelicals? and, What are the practical implications of your claim?

Some divisive inerrantists are fond of making dire predictions about what will happen if the church does not embrace inerrancy. I find these predictions hard to credit, for I see God at work in the world constantly creating new situations and new opportunities for his people. But rather than dispute these claims, let me counter with a dire prediction of my own. I say that truly alarming results will follow if divisive inerrancy gains wide acceptance in evangelical ranks. For it is plainly the case that many evangelical organizations— denominations, educational institutions, missionary groups, evangelistic enterprises, publishing houses, and religious periodicals—have both believers and nonbelievers in inerrancy in their employ. What would happen to the ministry of these organizations if the proposals of the divisive inerrantists were implemented?

I remember vividly a conversation I had recently

with an executive of a nationally known organization that works primarily with college students. Its staff includes both inerrantists and non-inerrantists. This person expressed dismay over the recent revival of the debate and especially the divisive stands that are being taken by some advocates of inerrancy. He said the people in his organization fear that the debate will split evangelicals and that if this happens, it may ruin their ministry. "What is your group going to do?" I asked. He said, "We are going to take no stand on the issue as an organization, proceed with our work, and hope the whole issue fades." I do not believe that the issue will fade—at least not in the near future. It is clear that there are those who are committed to keeping it alive. But I fervently join him in hoping, nonetheless.

How *do* we decide who is an evangelical and who is not? The short answer is that our criteria must be Biblical criteria, not essentially philosophical or apologetic notions such as inerrancy. The one book of the Bible that deals more than any other with the question of criteria for who is in the fellowship and who is not is the book of I John. I believe there are two criteria listed in I John. The first is Christological:

> By this you know the Spirit of God: every spirit which confesses that Jesus Christ has come in the flesh is of God, and every spirit which does not confess Jesus is not of God. (I John 4:2–3)

> Every one who believes that Jesus is the Christ is a child of God. (Ch. 5:1; cf. ch. 2:22–23)

> Whoever confesses that Jesus is the Son of God, God abides in him, and he in God. (Ch. 4:15)

The author is saying, I believe, that the relevant criteria are Christological criteria: he who believes in the incarnation (ch. 4:2–3), messiahship (ch. 5:1), and divinity of Jesus Christ (ch. 4:15) is a member of the fellowship of Christians. Those who do not are not. (See also I Cor. 15:1–4, where Paul claims that Christian affirmations about the death and resurrection of Christ are "of first importance.")

And the second criterion is practical or behavioral:

> By this we may be sure that we are in him: he who says he abides in him ought to walk in the same way in which he walked. (1 John 2:5–6)

> By this it may be seen who are the children of God, and who are the children of the devil: whoever does not do right is not of God, nor he who does not love his brother. (Ch. 3:10)

> Beloved, let us love one another; for love is of God, and he who loves is born of God and knows God. He who does not love does not know God; for God is love. (Ch. 4:7–8)

> By this we know that we love the children of God, when we love God and obey his commandments. For this is the love of God, that we keep his commandments. (Ch. 5:2–3)

So there is a practical criterion too. It is not enough just to have an orthodox theology. There are people who can sincerely affirm all the propositions in the classic creeds of the church but who have no living faith. What they intellectually affirm makes no practical difference in the way they live. An evangelical, then, is one who is orthodox in his Christology and who attempts to live out in his life the demands of his faith in Christ. "You will know them by their fruits," Jesus said (Matt. 7:20).

Thus it can be seen that I am not proposing my own view of the Bible as the criterion of who is an evangelical, as divisive inerrantists seem to me to be doing. I am not suggesting that everyone to the theological left of me is outside the pale.

How, then, do we decide which Christian doctrines are worth fighting over, so to speak, and which are not? For I too am troubled by the specter we sometimes see in liberal Protestantism—a broad and loose subjectivism wherein any theology at all is acceptable that is propounded by sincere people who call themselves Christian. But I am no sectarian either. Some fundamentalist Christians have shown far too much readiness to divide from other Christians at the drop of a hat, and I find this attitude unchristian. We must, of course, allow all human beings freedom to believe as they want to believe without interference or coercion. Still, lines must be drawn somewhere. Evangelical Christians must distinguish themselves theologically from nonevangelical Christians. So we must ask, Where are the lines to be drawn? I have no easy answer to this, only the flexible suggestion that those doctrines which are crucial to historic Christianity are worth fighting over, especially (but not exclusively) Christological doctrines such as those mentioned above. Some persons, as we have seen, think historic Christianity is at stake precisely at the point of Biblical inerrancy. I hope by now it is clear that this cannot be true. Even aside from the serious internal difficulties that plague the doctrine, inerrancy cannot be crucial to historic Christianity unless the epistemological argument and the slippery slide argument are sound, and they are not.

FINAL OBSERVATIONS

There are three final points that I want to discuss:

1. The first is not meant to be taken as an argument against inerrancy but is merely an expression of something of my attitude toward it. I believe that divisive inerrancy is a doctrine that is being pushed on us by an older generation of evangelicals. Inerrancy is a doctrine whose attractiveness we can perhaps understand in the context of the battles these people once had to fight against modernism, but I feel no need to fight these battles again. To be sure, I disagree with the assumptions that a good many nonevangelical theologians make about the Bible, and as situations call for it I have no hesitancy in making this known to them. But this older generation of evangelicals does not speak for me. I honor their commitment to God's word, but I feel no need to listen when they try to tell me what I must believe and the dire consequences that will follow if I don't.

Whatever truth there may be in this observation, I recognize that it cuts both ways. If I live long enough, I too will someday be part of "an older generation of evangelicals," and perhaps *my* theories will then be seen as outmoded. That is all right with me. God continues to work; the work of theology goes on. My ego is not involved in the hope that evangelicals at the turn of the next century believe exactly as I now be-

lieve. The Lord will be the same Lord, and the Bible
will still speak to them as God's word. If they have
that, plus a burning desire to do the will of God, they
will be all right.

2. To return to the present, unless all signs mislead,
these are heady days for Christian evangelicalism. The
religious momentum, at least in this country, is turning
in our favor. Our churches are growing. Our seminar-
ies are thriving. The Bible is being read. Evangelical
books are selling. People are paying attention to evangelicalism in a way that has not been true in decades.
In the Presidential campaign of 1976 the candidates of
both major parties were professing Christians who
energetically competed for "the evangelical vote."
What does the future hold for evangelicals? What does
God have in store for us? I do not know. But I do
strongly feel that the opportunities that are now ours
should not be wasted by sectarian bickering.

I am fully aware that divisive inerrantists are sincere
Christians who firmly believe that inerrancy is such a
watershed issue that it is worth division in evangelical
ranks. They will refuse to accept blame for the divisive
stands they feel they have had to take. They will say
the bickering is the fault of those Christians who do
not believe in inerrancy. Thus Francis Schaeffer, when
asked to respond to the charge that his strong insis-
tence on inerrancy is divisive, replied:

> I think Elijah gave the right answer when Ahab ac-
> cused him of being the troubler of Israel. The people
> who are taking a weak view of Scripture are the ones
> who are troubling evangelicalism today. I say this with

gentleness and love toward these people. The people who are making the difficulty are the people who have demoted Scripture from what it has been understood to be in the evangelical world until the fairly recent past.[68]

There are several questions that might be raised about this comment. Do evangelicals like me hold a "weak" view of Scripture? Have we "demoted" the Bible? Do we propose a less sturdy doctrine of Scripture than Christians have traditionally held? Certainly I am not prepared to grant that all Christians until fairly recently believed in inerrancy. Nor, even if it were true, that it necessarily follows from this that *we* must believe in inerrancy.

All that aside, it is clear Schaeffer feels that his strong stand on inerrancy is made necessary by the positions of people like me. The blame is ours, he is saying, not his. I will not debate this tiresome point of who is at fault in the present controversy. It would be a fruitless debate, and nobody could possibly win. My only response is a simple one. It is to ask divisive inerrantists to explain clearly and carefully, and in the light of arguments such as those I have presented in this book, why inerrancy is worth the price of division in evangelical ranks.

I most strongly believe that evangelicals need to stop bickering with each other. Our task is too great for us to waste our energy on technical intramural debates. We need to get on with what God has called us to do; we need to seize the opportunities he has placed before us. God calls us to worship him, to serve others, and to preach the saving grace of Christ to a spiritually hungry world. Of course, the work of theology must continue too. I believe it is crucial that evangelicals do theology, defining and defending the evangelical Christian position in lucid, compelling terms. But I also believe that the abandonment of divisive inerrancy by all evangelicals would be a good thing. It would help us present a united front to the world and would enable us to get about our business.

3. The motto of this book, on the epigraph page, is provided by one of the prescribed questions that was addressed to me at my ordination to the ministry in 1965. Whole generations of Presbyterian and Reformed ordinands have had to answer this question. The conviction that the Bible is "the only infallible rule of faith and practice" is an old and revered one. What did those who first used the expression mean by it? I think they meant something like this: The whole Bible, when correctly interpreted, leads those who believe and obey into the religious truth that sets people free; the Bible can and does lead people to a knowledge of God as he has revealed himself to us in Jesus Christ. So the affirmation is about the message of the whole Bible when correctly interpreted, not about isolated passages or claims. These, standing alone or interpreted incorrectly, can indeed lead to religious error. For example, Christians believe that the ceremonial law of Leviticus must be interpreted in the light of the New Testament, especially Galatians and Hebrews, lest it lead people to legalism. This is what I took the question that was addressed to me in 1965 to mean, and this book is a way of recommending that Christians today make the same affirmation.

People like Lindsell seem to believe that inability to

affirm inerrancy leads people into theological liberalism. But I do not agree with this. Stated in this way, the point is at least vastly oversimplified. Like anyone else who has studied theology in recent years, I have read the works of many liberal theologians. Living as I do in a town that can boast of four undergraduate departments of religion, one graduate department of religion, and one well-known nonevangelical seminary, I can say that I am personally acquainted with many liberal Christian theologians. Unless I am badly mistaken, what leads these people to their theological convictions is most definitely not their belief that there are historical and scientific errors in the Bible. Most of my liberal friends apparently don't care to become involved in debates over inerrancy. My own diagnosis is this: What leads them to liberalism, apart from cultural or personal issues, is their acceptance of certain philosophical or scientific assumptions that are inimical to evangelical theology—e.g., assumptions about what is "believable to modern people," "consistent with modern science," "acceptable by twentieth-century canons of scholarship," and the like.

What moral, if any, is to be drawn from this? I think if we want to convince people of the superiority of evangelicalism, the way to do it is not to try desperately to show that the Bible is errorless. Rather, we must try to get people to see the superiority of the Biblical world view. We must try to get them to accept Biblical rather than non-Biblical assumptions: in a word, to place themselves under the theological authority of the Bible. Evangelical Christians are called upon to do many things these days. From time to time we are called upon to defend evangelicalism against the criticisms of liberal theologians. At other times we are called upon to answer the simple questions of spiritually hungry people who long to know God. In both cases, as it seems to me, our task is to convince people not that the Bible is inerrant but that it is the only infallible rule of faith and practice.

NOTES

1. Archibald Alexander Hodge and Benjamin B. Warfield, "Inspiration," *The Presbyterian Review,* Vol. II (1881). Cited in Richard J. Coleman, "Biblical Inerrancy: Are We Going Anywhere?" *Theology Today,* Vol. XXXI, No. 4 (Jan. 1975), p. 300.

2. Lindsell's theory is found in his book *The Battle for the Bible* (Zondervan Publishing House, 1976).

3. Fuller's theory is found in his articles "The Nature of Biblical Inerrancy," *Journal of the American Scientific Affiliation,* June 1972, and "Benjamin B. Warfield's View of Faith and History," *Bulletin of the Evangelical Theological Society,* Vol. XI, No. 2 (Spring 1968).

4. See Lindsell, *Battle,* pp. 13, 23, 139, 210, 25, 206. Lindsell claims that his book is irenical rather than polemical in nature (p. 24), but this is hard to support from the text. He sees inerrancy as a "battle" (pp. 13, 26, 200) that must be fought despite the risk of division in evangelical ranks (p. 25).

5. *Ibid.,* pp. 27n., 36, 31.

6. *Ibid.,* p. 18.

7. *Ibid.,* pp. 34–35, 40, 162, 171, 182.

8. *Ibid.,* pp. 19, 41–71.

9. *Ibid.,* pp. 33, 39, 114, 132, 201, 203, 210.

10. *Ibid.,* pp. 24, 25, 104, 120–121, 139, 142, 148, 154–155, 157, 176, 183, 196, 203, 206, 210.

11. *Ibid.,* p. 203.

12. *Ibid.,* pp. 36–37.

13. *Ibid.,* p. 168. Cf. also pp. 163, 165.

14. *Ibid.,* pp. 163, 168–169, 172.

15. There is an argument in Lindsell's chapter on the phenomena that will startle anyone who is trained in logic. Lindsell writes: "Paul says, 'If you confess with your lips that Jesus is Lord and believe in your heart that God raised him from the dead, you will be saved' (Rom. 10:9). The converse of any proposition is true. Thus, 'If you do not call Jesus Lord and do not believe in your heart that God raised him from the dead, you will not be saved' " (p. 178). It is difficult to know what to say about an argument of this sort. In the first place, it is not clear to me what Lindsell means by the "converse" of a proposition. Perhaps he means the proposition that results from negating both the antecedent and the consequent of a hypothetical statement. But even if this is what he means, where does he get the strange doctrine that "the converse of any proposition is true"? Perhaps he means that the converse of any *true* (hypothetical) statement is true. But this is a dubious doctrine, to say the least. For suppose that this is a true hypothetical statement, as I believe it is: "If Jones was born in the U.S.A., Jones is an American." Then the "converse" must be: "If Jones was not born in the U.S.A., Jones is not an American." But this need not be true at all—Jones might be a naturalized citizen who was born in Wales.

16. Lindsell, *Battle,* p. 39. Nor have any historical or archaeological discoveries exposed errors in Scripture, according to Lindsell. See p. 35.

17. *Ibid.,* pp. 174–176.

18. See *ibid.,* pp. 161, 169.

19. Fuller, "Inerrancy," p. 50.

20. *Ibid.,* p. 47. Cf. pp. 49, 50.

21. *Ibid.,* pp. 47, 50.

22. *Ibid.,* pp. 48, 47, 50. Cf. Fuller, "Warfield," p. 81.

23. *Ibid.,* p. 48. Cf. Fuller, "Warfield," pp. 77–80.

24. *Ibid.,* p. 50.

25. Cited in Fuller, "Warfield," pp. 75–76.

26. Fuller, "Inerrancy," p. 50. See also Fuller, "Warfield," pp. 75, 77, 80, 81, and Daniel P. Fuller, "On Revelation and Biblical Authority," *Journal of the Evangelical Theological Society,* Vol. XVI, No. 2 (Spring 1973), pp. 67–69.

27. See John W. Montgomery, "Biblical Inerrancy: What Is at Stake?" *God's Inerrant Word,* ed. by John W. Montgomery (Bethany Fellowship, Inc., 1974), pp. 32, 42.

28. Fuller, "On Revelation," pp. 68–69.

29. Fuller, "Inerrancy," p. 49.

30. Fuller, "Warfield," p. 81.

31. Fuller, "On Revelation," p. 68. Cf. Fuller, "Inerrancy," p. 50.

32. Fuller, "Inerrancy," p. 50.

33. Fuller, "Warfield," p. 83.

34. Everett F. Harrison, "The Phenomena of Scripture," in *Revelation and the Bible,* ed. by Carl F. H. Henry (Baker Book House, 1958), p. 238.

35. See, e.g., Lindsell, *Battle,* pp. 40, 162, 182.

36. Harold Lindsell, "The Infallible Word," *Christianity Today,* Aug. 25, 1972, p. 11. See also R. C. Sproul, "The Case for Inerrancy: A Methodological Analysis," in Montgomery (ed.), *God's Inerrant Word,* p. 257; Clark H. Pinnock, *Biblical Revelation* (Moody Press, 1971), pp. 70, 73. And Harrison says that inerrancy "is a natural corollary of full inspiration," in Henry (ed.), *Revelation and the Bible,* p. 250.

37. Daniel P. Fuller, "Evangelicalism and Biblical Inerrancy" (unpublished), p. 17.

38. I owe this point to Sidney Chapman, "Bahnsen on Inspiration," *The Evangelical Quarterly,* Vol. XLVII (1975), p. 167.

39. Lindsell, *Battle,* pp. 201, 203; Fuller, "Inerrancy," p. 50; Fuller, "On Revelation," p. 68; Pinnock, *Biblical Revelation,* pp. 59, 73; Clark H. Pinnock, "Limited Inerrancy: A Critical Appraisal and Constructive Alternative," in Montgomery (ed.), *God's Inerrant Word,* p. 156.

40. Lindsell, *Battle,* pp. 39, 201, 203, 210.

41. *Ibid.,* pp. 33, 114, 132, 203; Pinnock, *Biblical Revelation,* p. 80.

42. Lindsell, *Battle,* p. 210.

43. René Descartes, *Meditations and Selections from the Principles of Philosophy* (The Open Court Publishing Company, 1946), p. 22.

44. Carl F. H. Henry, "Conflict Over Biblical Inerrancy,"

Christianity Today, May 7, 1976, p. 25. Henry is a believer in inerrancy, but I would like to say that I admire and appreciate his attitude toward the current debate.

45. Francis A. Schaeffer, *No Final Conflict* (Inter-Varsity Press, 1976), p. 24.

46. Cited in Lindsell, *Battle,* p. 54.

47. *Ibid.,* p. 36.

48. Edward J. Carnell, *The Case for Orthodox Theology* (The Westminster Press, 1959), p. 99.

49. Among other forms of the SSA, this seems to be the argument of Lindsell in *The Battle for the Bible.* See pp. 139, 142–143, 159–160. See also pp. 24, 25, 104, 120–121, 148, 154–155, 157, 176, 179, 183, 196, 203, 206, and 210.

50. The only thing even remotely similar that I know of is Paul's claim that he who violates even one precept of the Old Testament law violates the whole law (Gal. 3:10; see also James 2:10), but this is obviously a different matter.

51. Lindsell, *Battle,* p. 169.

52. *Ibid.*

53. Pinnock, *Biblical Revelation,* p. 76.

54. Carnell, *The Case for Orthodox Theology,* pp. 98–99.

55. Harrison, "The Phenomena of Scripture," in Henry (ed.), *Revelation and the Bible,* p. 244.

56. See, e.g., Montgomery, "Biblical Inerrancy: What Is at Stake?" in Montgomery (ed.), *God's Inerrant Word,* p. 38. See also Lindsell, *Battle,* p. 171.

57. Harrison, "The Phenomena of Scripture," in Henry (ed.), *Revelation and the Bible,* p. 249.

58. James Orr, *Revelation and Inspiration* (Baker Book House, 1969; originally published 1910), pp. 197–198.

59. Cited in Troy Organ, "Brother, Are You Saved? or How to Handle the Religious Census Taker," *The Christian Century,* Vol. XCII, No. 33 (Oct. 15, 1975), p. 897.

60. Lindsell, *Battle,* pp. 161–162.

61. *Ibid.,* pp. 169; 159–160. See also pp. 176, 179, 183.

62. Here and elsewhere in this book I have been influenced by George E. Ladd, *The New Testament and Criticism* (Wm. B. Eerdmans Publishing Company, 1967).

63. For a more thorough expression of the relation of evidence and reason to religious faith, see my forthcoming book, *Faith, Skepticism, and Evidence,* to be published by Bucknell University Press.

64. I agree with Walter Wink on this point. See Walter Wink, *The Bible in Human Transformation* (Fortress Press, 1973), pp. 1–15.

65. G. C. Berkouwer, *Holy Scripture* (Wm. B. Eerdmans Publishing Company, 1975), p. 265.

66. Montgomery, "Biblical Inerrancy: What Is at Stake?" in Montgomery (ed.), *God's Inerrant Word,* p. 26.

67. *Ibid.,* p. 29.

68. Francis Schaeffer, *Christianity Today,* Oct. 8, 1976, p. 25.

BIBLIOGRAPHY

Barr, James. *The Bible in the Modern World.* Harper & Row, Publishers, Inc., 1973.

Beegle, Dewey. *Scripture, Tradition, and Authority.* Wm. B. Eerdmans Publishing Company, 1973.

———. *The Inspiration of Scripture.* The Westminster Press, 1963.

Carnell, Edward J. *The Case for Orthodox Theology.* The Westminster Press, 1959.

Chapman, Sidney. "Bahnsen on Inspiration," *The Evangelical Quarterly,* Vol. XLVII (1975).

Coleman, Richard J. "Biblical Inerrancy: Are We Going Anywhere?" *Theology Today,* Vol. XXXI, No. 4 (Jan. 1975).

Fuller, Daniel P. "Benjamin B. Warfield's View of Faith and History," *Bulletin of the Evangelical Theological Society,* Vol. XI, No. 2 (Spring 1968).

———. "Evangelicalism and Biblical Inerrancy." Unpublished.

———. "The Nature of Biblical Inerrancy," *Journal of the American Scientific Affiliation,* June 1972.

————. "On Revelation and Biblical Authority," *Journal of the Evangelical Theological Society,* Vol. XVI, No. 2 (Spring 1973).

Harrison, Everett F. "The Phenomena of Scripture." In *Revelation and the Bible,* ed. by Carl F. H. Henry. Baker Book House, 1958.

Henry, Carl F. H. "Conflict Over Biblical Inerrancy," *Christianity Today,* May 7, 1976.

Hodge, Archibald Alexander, and Warfield, Benjamin B. "Inspiration," *The Presbyterian Review,* Vol. II, No. 6 (April 1881).

Jewett, Paul K. *Man as Male and Female.* Wm. B. Eerdmans Publishing Company, 1975.

Ladd, George E. *The New Testament and Criticism.* Wm. B. Eerdmans Publishing Company, 1967.

Lindsell, Harold. *The Battle for the Bible.* Zondervan Publishing House, 1976.

————. "The Infallible Word," *Christianity Today,* Aug. 25, 1972.

Montgomery, John W. "Biblical Inerrancy: What Is at Stake?" In *God's Inerrant Word,* ed. by John W. Montgomery. Bethany Fellowship, Inc., 1974.

Orr, James. *Revelation and Inspiration.* Baker Book House, 1969; originally published 1910.

Pache, René. *The Inspiration and Authority of the Bible.* Moody Press, 1969.

Packer, J. I. *Fundamentalism and the Word of God.* Wm. B. Eerdmans Publishing Company, 1958.

Pinnock, Clark H. *Biblical Revelation.* Moody Press, 1971.

————. "Limited Inerrancy: A Critical Appraisal and Constructive Alternative." In *God's Inerrant Word,* ed. by John W. Montgomery. Bethany Fellowship, Inc., 1974.

Reid, John K. S. *The Authority of Scripture.* London: Methuen & Company, 1957.

Schaeffer, Francis A. *No Final Conflict.* Inter-Varsity Press, 1976.

Smart, James. *The Interpretation of Scripture.* The Westminster Press, 1961.

Sproul, R. C. "The Case for Inerrancy: A Methodological Analysis." In *God's Inerrant Word,* ed. by John W. Montgomery. Bethany Fellowship, Inc., 1974.

Stonehouse, N. B., and Woolley, Paul (eds.). *The Infallible Word.* Wm. B. Eerdmans Publishing Company, 1953.

Young, Edward J. *Thy Word Is Truth.* Wm. B. Eerdmans Publishing Company, 1957.